# Life 2 the Full

**Raymond Floodgate**

authorHOUSE®

*AuthorHouse™ UK*
*1663 Liberty Drive*
*Bloomington, IN 47403  USA*
*www.authorhouse.co.uk*
*Phone: 0800.197.4150*

*Published by AuthorHouse  02/09/2017*

*ISBN: 978-1-5246-6154-0 (sc)*
*ISBN: 978-1-5246-6155-7 (hc)*
*ISBN: 978-1-5246-6153-3 (e)*

# Contents

# Chapter 1

# Living Life to the Full

"Living life to the full" means different things to different people. For most of us, it means holding down a job that will support our family's wants and needs. Many of us get only one day off a week to relax, pursue an activity or hobby, do the weekly shopping, visit relatives and friends, or catch up with the latest film at the cinema. We might think that with all of our social activities and household chores, our lives are as full as they can get. Anyway, the TV is on now, so it's time to chill out.

That is not living life to the full.

An empty life will always appear to be full if it is cluttered with trivia, meaningless activities, and gossip. You need to fill the space you occupy with thoughts and activities that have purpose and will help you grow as a person who will progress to greater things.

Gossip is the scourge of modern-day society. Almost anyone can become a victim. Beware the so-called "friend" who whispers behind your back. Gossip doesn't even have to be true. A rumour will suffice – just as long as it creates the right impact on delivery and starts the wheels turning. It then takes on a life of its own as it moves from person to person. Your reputation and credibility can be torn to shreds with just one quick and wicked wag of the tongue – but, never fear, retribution is not far away from the vengeful tongue of the gossip. No one can hide from the universal law of karma: "As you sow, so shall you reap."

Gossiping is not one of the requirements for living life to the full. You should fill the space you occupy with things that will help you to grow as a person. Do not gossip about other people; you are only hurting yourself and may hold back your own development and progress.

It has been said that most people spend more time planning their holiday than planning their life. You can spend many hours planning for one and months or years saving your money. It can consume hours, days, and even months of thought energy. More often than not, when the time arrives, your expectations are running high. This can create quite a stressful occasion.

Before you know it, the two- or three-week holiday in the sun is over – in what seems like the twinkling of an eye – and you are left wondering where the time went. You start to pack your bags for the long journey home, and then the tension sets in again. As you make your way back to the airport, you mentally prepare yourself for the return to work and the mundane pace of your normal life.

A holiday is an adventure that takes us out of what is considered our "normal" life. Many hope that going on holiday will somehow change the whole of their life for the better, but it doesn't. It is just a holiday. It lasts a week or two and then lingers on in the head for another couple of weeks. This is not living life to the full.

Such recreational events make up only a small part of your life. They're not worth the amount of time or energy that is spent preparing for them, and they're not worth the time and energy that is spent afterwards thinking about and trying to relive them. Holidays are absolutely a part of our life (and a very necessary part at that), but they should be put into perspective. They should not be regarded as the be-all and end-all of life. Put more energy into filling the space you occupy on a day-to-day basis; this will help you to grow as a person so you can progress to greater things.

Living life to the full doesn't mean that you must cram as much as you can into every minute of every day. You should only do every day whatever is comfortable for you. Never do *too* much: filling your day with too much work, too many activities, and even too much rest brings you into the realm of extremes. This can lead to all kinds of problems, both mental and physical. Always take the middle way and stay within the parameters of common sense. To do anything to excess repeatedly will put great strain upon your body and mind. If this is not checked, it can cause your body to start to break down – and that is definitely *not* living life to the full.

If you start to break down, either mentally or physically, ill health can set in. This quickly impairs your ability to complete the tasks that you intend to complete during your stay on earth. The tasks that I refer to are the lessons that were set for you when you were preparing to come to this world.

Shortening your life by self-infliction is no excuse for not completing the lessons you came here to learn. Your physical body has a self-healing mechanism built in; it is quite able to repair itself and will keep working way beyond the lifespan that

3

has been allotted to you for completing your lessons. Living life to the full means achieving, successfully, the activities that need to be completed and learned for that day. Do not put in so much effort that your mind and body come under pressure. There is no need to make your life uncomfortable.

Only do the right amount of work for today; there is no need to do more. Do not try to do tomorrow's activities today. Do not try to catch up on the things that you should have done yesterday. You will only upset the balance within yourself, and this may cause you problems in the future. To live life to the full, you only need to fill the space you occupy with the right amount of thoughts and the right amount of activities. This will help you grow as a person so you may progress to greater things.

It is important to stay healthy while you are on this world. Living life to the full is the way to achieve this. Unfortunately, we live in a society that does not promote health; it is more focused on making money, and several industries rely on people becoming ill so they have to buy medication to remedy their illnesses (many of which are the product of other industries). This only solves one problem, and that is the one that interests the pharmaceutical, chemical, and food industries: how to make money. They make huge amounts of money, but people are still ill.

Generally, people do not need large amounts of medication. What they need is education. They need to learn about prevention rather than prescriptions. This mentality of waiting for things to go wrong so that they can be fixed seems to apply to most things, and it most certainly applies to the health of the world population. We live in a world that relies on drug-related remedies to treat illnesses. This type of regimen does not get to the root of the problem; it only treats the symptoms.

When one lives life to the full, there is no illness. The truth of this statement will become more apparent as you read further into this book.

It is claimed by experts from various good lifestyle organisations that healthy eating, maintaining a good exercise regimen, and thinking and acting in a positive manner will increase longevity. While all of these activities are essential to living a healthy life, not one of them will increase the length of your life by even one minute over the time that has been already allotted to you. Living life to the full includes all of the fields of activity and more. None of them can make you live *longer*, but each of them can help you to live *better*. You can create a healthier, fitter, and mentally stronger life right up to the day you die, and that is a fact. To live your life to the full, you must fill the space you occupy. This will help you grow as a person and progress to greater things.

## Exercise

It is true that exercise is good for the body and mind. There are many kinds of exercises that you can do to help maintain your health and fitness. Many of these are done by top athletes all over the world. They are recommended by sports scientists and health experts to the populations of all nations worldwide – and rightly so. But the correct exercise is best.

When you do the correct exercise, the benefits far outweigh any benefits that you might obtain from all other forms of exercise. I will be explaining what exercise is the correct exercise in a later chapter. For now, just understand that the correct exercise is one of the components needed to live life to the full and help you to fill the space you occupy so that you can grow as a person and progress to greater things.

## Food

It may be in a book or on TV – even films are being made about food, from the humble burger to gourmet food and everything in between – but all over the world, food presenters tell us what we should and shouldn't eat. They all seem to have their own ideas about what is best for us, but the correct food is best. The correct food is one of the components needed to live life to the full.

It is important that you eat a balanced toxin-free diet. You may find that, to get a toxin-free diet, you have to travel further afield when shopping. It is unlikely that you will get what you need from the average supermarket. When you look at what supermarkets are selling in more detail, you may find that, although they offer a large variety of food products that are supposed to fill your daily dietary needs, many of these products fall short of this requirement. You may also realise after a little more investigation that supermarkets are not so "super" after all.

The correct food is the best food. It will give you all the vitamins, minerals, proteins, fibre, and amino acids your body requires. The correct food will help you to regulate your weight, and it will be toxin-free. I will be writing more about correct food in a later chapter. Correct food coupled with the correct exercise are two of the components that will help you live life to the full.

## Energy

We get energy from eating the correct foods. We also get energy from practising the correct exercise. So what is this energy I am talking about? This energy is called *chi* or life-force energy. Chi is everywhere, just like the air we breathe – except that the air we breathe is confined to a thin band or layer around the earth, whereas chi resides in the whole of the universe and beyond.

Chi is seated at the atomic level within your body. Without chi, you would not be able to sustain life and neither would any other living thing. Chi is the most important and precious substance in the universe, and it is used by the innate intelligence within our body to self-heal. Our body is under attack every day, and self-healing with chi takes place twenty-four hours a day every day. Chi will protect us from any disease or illness that may be present within us. If chi is healing us each minute of every day, then why is it that we still get ill? I shall explain this at a later stage in this book.

You replenish your body with chi every time you breathe. Chi is also being replaced when you eat the correct food and also when you do the correct exercises. Knowing the importance of chi and the role it plays in not only our lives but the life of the whole universe, I am surprised how few people know about its existence – most especially those people who are in positions within our society where having this knowledge could make a difference.

## Breathing

We all breathe the air that is around us. It is obviously something that must be done for life to continue on this planet. Knowing how important breathing is, I am amazed to find that very few people do it correctly. As many as 95 per cent of people who I have been associated with over the years tend to "shallow-breathe". Shallow-breathing will keep you alive, but it is not the *correct* method of breathing.

Shallow-breathing is the lazy way of breathing – although, in the long run, it takes more effort to do. When you shallow-breathe, you deny your body the correct amount of oxygen for it to function properly. The lack of oxygen will starve some, if not all, of the organs in your body of their full quota of fuel, thus affecting their performance. When the organs in your body are not getting the correct amount of oxygen or the right amount of chi, then over a long period of time they will start to develop problems and will eventually break down.

This fact must be known by professional people in this area of expertise, but when I ask students in my classes who have suffered with diseased organs, and others who have respiratory problems, whether they have been given instruction for correct breathing either by hospital consultants or by their GP, the answer is always no. Instead, in the case of those with respiratory problems, they have been given an inhaler to help them breathe.

I am not saying that giving out drugs to people who need them is not necessary, but surely one must look at a remedy that does not include taking drugs first, especially something as simple as the instruction of correct breathing. Correct breathing is another component that will help you to live life to the full, and it will also enable you to fill the space you occupy and grow as a person to progress to greater things. I will describe the correct way of breathing later in this book.

## Relaxation

Relaxation is not something that comes naturally to most people. To some, it doesn't come at all. It is a difficult subject to teach, as relaxing means one thing to some people and something totally different to others. When all is said and done, when one is relaxed, one is relaxed. You are either relaxed or you are not. Total relaxation has to be worked on by everyone – but when you get it and can master it, it never leaves you.

You can sit in a chair with your feet up drinking a glass of wine and feel quite comfortable, but that's not relaxation. You will know when you are truly relaxed because it is unmistakeable; there is nothing like it. *Correct* relaxation is the only relaxation there is. Any other meaning of the word is not relaxation; it is something else. When there is true and correct relaxation, you may find that things will generally run smoother in your life. When you are truly relaxed, whatever it is that you want from life will come to you with less effort. The correct method of relaxation is another component that will help you live life to the full.

## Stress

Cardiovascular disease is the biggest killer of humans in the Western world. This is a fact that is widely talked about in the published reports of the medical industry. We eat too much of the wrong foods. We have a diet full of fat, starch, and sugar, and as a nation we consume more processed food than we should while going without the fresh healthy food that the body needs. We all know this, so why do we do it?

Cancer is the second most frequently reported killer in the Western world. There is a list of ailments as long as your arm that also has scary statistics to go with them. These ailments always have one thing in common: They all have the same cause, and that cause is *stress*. It doesn't matter what the disease is called, there is always only one cause, and that is stress. If you treat your body and your mind as if they are not worth anything, then guess what, that is exactly what they will end up being worth. Respect your mind by thinking in the correct manner. Respect your body by giving it the correct nourishment and by doing the correct exercise. You will remain fit and healthy right up until the day you leave here.

Stress will unbalance your body and mind. It is the biggest killer because it is the cause of all illness and disease. It is not the symptom. By eating the wrong foods, you put the organs that have the job of digesting that food under stress. By doing the wrong exercise, you are putting the muscles, tendons, and ligaments affected by that exercise under stress. When you think incorrect thoughts, you put your mind under stress. When you are able to eliminate stress from every part of your life, you will be opening the way to leading a better, healthier life. Don't miss this opportunity. Be aware of what this book is offering you. Read the rest of it and practice what you read. Then you too will be able to live life to the full.

## Egotistic behaviour

When you have thoughts of your own grandeur (and this is an excellent example of incorrect thinking) and place yourself above all others in your mind, it is very rare that anything you dream will come to fruition outside of your head. Egotism is a quality that must be conquered if progress is to take place in this life. How on earth can you help those in need while your mind is so engrossed with its own self-importance? Get rid of egotistical behaviour by adjusting your thoughts. Correct thinking is best. When the mind is thinking correctly, this can lead you to a life being lived to the full.

So far in this book, I have mentioned some of the things you might want to take a look at in your own life. In the remaining chapters, I aim to show you how to live your life to the full, should you want to. This will also help you to fill the space that you occupy so that you can grow as a person and progress to greater things.

## Change is possible

Can you imagine yourself living a life in which the common cold does not exist and all major diseases and illnesses no longer occur in the body or in the mind? Can you imagine yourself at 40 or 50 or 60 or 70 years old feeling like you're still 25? Friends, relatives, and acquaintances who are about the same age as you start taking shorter steps when they walk and their back starts hunching slightly, but your strides are long and your back is straight, your muscles are strong and your joints are flexible. Your mind is sharp and alert while those of a similar age to you are starting to dither and be forgetful.

When you can be aware of the way you are in your world and notice how others are in their world, it may concern you a little to see the people you know and love beginning to deteriorate before your eyes. That's when you realise that you are living life to the full, and that is the difference between you and those around you.

Living life to the full is not some mysterious process. Once you know about it, it is obvious. It has always been there, but you probably didn't think to look. It is not something that is taught in schools; even our teachers have not been taught it. It is not a part of the curriculum at any level of education, so why should you know about it? Our society has totally overlooked this way of living and opted for the "get more money and grab everything you can" type of existence. However, when you live life to the full, your life becomes rich and abundant in every way. All of this can be obtained with very little effort on your part.

The society you currently live in associates wealth with money and possessions – a very narrow view of what wealth truly is. Money and possessions are absolutely a part of wealth, but only a small part. When you live life to the full, every aspect of living is taken into account. Unfortunately, at the moment in our current society, there are many facets of living that we are not informed about. I am not saying that this information is blatantly withheld from us; in fact, I have come to believe over the years of studying for this book that there are very few people who are actually aware of this information anyway. This could be the very reason why our society is the way it is.

I firmly believe that things cannot go on this way for very much longer. There is evidence to suggest that flaws have already started to appear. The health of the nation is in a state of deterioration. The health of the financial sector, not only in the UK but throughout Europe and America, is slowly collapsing and may be coming to a head soon. Crime is at an all-time high, and the stress level of our society is almost at a breaking point.

So what can be done to turn things around? How can we lift ourselves out of the mess we are in? How can we get those who have the power to take action to put in place the changes that are needed to make our society a safer, richer, and happier place for everyone?

We can't. That will never happen. It will never happen because the people who can make a difference are the same people who are only in it for power and money. Power and money for themselves, that is – not for us. If the people in power can't or won't do it, then how can we as ordinary people effect such a change? By living life to the full and taking on the responsibility for our own well-being.

Throughout the rest of this book, I will show you how you can live life to the full. I firmly believe that if only 40 per cent of the population of the UK were to follow these suggestions and actually live their life to the full, they would rock the foundations of society – so much so that it would force change to happen. If 40 per cent of people were healthy and had no need to go to the doctor or into hospital, the pharmaceutical companies who supply the drugs to these institutions would experience a 40 per cent reduction in income. If this could be emulated by people in other countries throughout Europe and America, governments would be forced to change the way they think about the health and well-being of their people.

Just suppose that 40 per cent of people in the UK refused to eat crops that had been sprayed with chemical poisons and would eat only non-toxic organic crops. This would turn the farming industry and the food suppliers upside down, and if this trend was emulated throughout Europe and America, then agricultural policies would have to be rewritten to accommodate the growing number of people who refuse to be poisoned by their food. This can easily be achieved when you make the decision to change from your current lifestyle and adopt the way of living your life to the full.

Living life to the full at first glance may seem like a lot of effort, but then so does dragging yourself along to see the doctor when you are not feeling well. It is not much fun sitting in a waiting room full of sick people for twenty minutes or so because if you weren't ill when you went in, you certainly will be when you come out. Unfortunately, this is what happens when you live in a society of stress and competition – where the essence of life to the full is not lived.

Do you ever feel bloated and too full when you have just eaten? Have you noticed that you have put on a little more weight recently and are feeling a bit sluggish when moving around? Are you more tired than you used to be? Is this is a regular occurrence? With just a small change to your lifestyle, you need never feel this way again. Once you accept that a change is needed, you are halfway there.

Read the rest of this book and take on board what it is saying to you. If you have the courage to take the action required and follow the guidelines laid down, changes in your life will start to occur. It will take a little effort from you, but the benefit you receive will far outweigh the effort you have to put in. This is life-changing information, and once you have adopted these suggested guidelines into your life, change will be inevitable. It should be a life change for the better.

# Chapter 2

# Breathing

Breathing is the single most important thing we all do in life. So it is quite surprising how many of us do not do it properly. From my experience in this field, I have found that almost all of the students who have attended my classes or clients who have visited my treatment therapy room breathe incorrectly.

Breathing is a natural and automatic process. It has to be. If we had to manage the breathing process by ourselves, it would take up so much of our time that we wouldn't get anything else done. Having said that, we do have some limited ability to influence the breathing process, and most of us influence it by what can only be called the least line of resistance.

The method most people choose to use is the top breathing technique, also known as shallow breathing. This way of breathing is okay inasmuch as it will keep you alive, but it is not the most efficient or healthiest method of breathing. There will be noticeable side effects when this type of breathing is adopted. The first thing that may become apparent is the number of times you have to breathe in and out compared to a person who uses the correct breathing technique.

The reason for this is because when the shallow breathing method is used, only the top half of the lungs is being filled with air when you inhale. This means that there will not be enough air taken in to supply the whole of the body with the amount of oxygen and chi that it needs. The shallow breather will always have to breathe more often to try to fulfil the body's oxygen and chi requirements.

When breathing in this fashion, the body is forced to use a different set of muscles, which can make the shoulders go up and down every time you breathe. The diaphragm is the muscle that assists the action of breathing, but with the shallow breathing method the diaphragm is hardly used at all. In fact, the diaphragm's movement when shallow-breathing is in reverse, which reduces the capacity of the lungs so that only the top half of the lungs can fill with air. (This is in no way related to the reverse abdominal breathing exercise.) This style of breathing can become very tiring and is a possible cause of stress from a stiff neck, headache, aching shoulders, and a dull mind.

The short supply of oxygen and chi delivered by shallow breathing can have a detrimental effect on the internal organs of the body if it is not checked. When the organs are short-changed of the fuel they need to function properly, they will be placed under stress. Too much stress for long periods of time results in a breakdown. I don't mean that they will stop working altogether immediately; they will probably carry on working for years even if you remain a shallow breather. But they will eventually succumb to disease, mainly because of the long periods of stress that they have had to endure.

When this point is reached, the organs will stop working – or, if the cellular replacement process is affected by prolonged stress and lack of chi and oxygen, the organs' cellular structure could becomes cancerous. Then *you* may stop working. It is something worth thinking about.

The brain is an important part of the body that relies on a full supply of oxygen and chi. It is said that after four minutes without oxygen, the brain will cease to function properly and will eventually die. So it is extremely important that there is a constant and uninterrupted supply of oxygen and chi to the brain to maintain not only your health but also the continuation of your life.

When you shallow-breathe and the brain is deprived of its full quota of oxygen and chi, certain side effects occur. A lack of concentration is most certainly a symptom of low oxygen levels in the brain. The brain will be under stress at this point because of the short supply of fuel, and it will be unable to make quick decisions to solve any problems that may occur. Panic attacks are also associated with low levels of oxygen in the brain. The mind gets confused and decides on a course of action that will seem perfectly normal to the person having the panic attack but, in reality, appears bizarre and out of the ordinary to friends and onlookers. Sometimes the problems associated with this kind of stress become so overwhelming that they drive the sufferer into depression. Eventually, if stretched beyond the breaking point, that person may take his or her own life.

When we are born, we breathe correctly – that is to say, we use the diaphragm when breathing and take in the right amount of air so that the body can grow normally and function properly. When we get older, for reasons unknown, our breathing changes. Maybe it is because laziness sets in when we are in our youth and we just can't be bothered to breathe properly; or perhaps our lives become so busy when we are older that we just don't have the time to take in a full breath. Many women actually hold their breath when they are concentrating, which must surely affect their level of concentration.

Whatever the reason for not breathing properly, the consequences are always the same and plain to see. Our body no longer functions properly, and our attitude towards life changes. For many, this means going through life with little confidence and low self-esteem. For others, shallow breathing means low concentration levels and reduced problem-solving abilities. For everyone who breathes in this way, the main cause of suffering will be the stress that shallow-breathing brings to them. When the body does not receive its full quota of oxygen and chi, any part that relies on oxygen and chi to work properly will be affected, which of course is *every* part.

The whole of the body will be put under stress, and stress is a potential killer. Stress is the cause of whatever disease you will eventually die from, whether it is heart disease, cancer, respiratory disease, or diseases of the liver, pancreas, or kidney. The list goes on. If we put any part of the body under stress by starving it of its life-giving fuel (oxygen and chi), then it will eventually break down. So what is the solution? Breathe correctly.

We can always find somebody or something to blame for our troubles, but at the end of the day, the responsibility for our health is ours alone. The solution is therefore in our own hands. Learn how to breathe properly and eliminate stress from your life.

**Breathing correctly**

When we breathe correctly, the breath moves slowly in and out of the lungs and the lungs become fully inflated and completely deflated. Also, when we breathe correctly, our body uses a completely different set of muscles compared to those of a shallow-breather. The diaphragm, which is immediately below the rib cage and to the front centre of the body, is the muscle that is used to assist correct breathing. There are many breathing exercises that can be done and which are used in various group activities; some of them use the diaphragm and some do not. These are breathing exercises and are normally done for a specific reason. They should not be confused with correct breathing. Correct breathing is the breathing that we do to stay alive, and it should be done at all times.

When we breathe correctly, our objective is to totally fill the lungs with air so as to maintain the continuous and smooth running of all of the vital organs in the body. Failure to do this will result in problems. There are many benefits that can be had when we take on, and understand, the process of correct breathing. Breathing correctly will affect every part of the body, from the brain right down to the feet, and is therefore vital for the well-being of the whole body.

The cells of the body require oxygen and chi to stay healthy, and when they reach the end of their effective lifetime, they are replaced by new cells. If the old cells have been treated well and are healthy, then the ones that replace them will be healthy too. Every part of the body structure is made up of cells, and there are many different jobs that cells undertake throughout the body. Some of these cells will be used to construct the liver, while other different kinds of cells will be used to make up the kidneys or perhaps the bones. All of the cells in the body, no matter what they are used for, require oxygen and chi to be healthy.

Unhealthy cells that have been denied the full amount of oxygen and chi may be replaced when their life expectancy is reached by new cells that could, themselves, become defective, because the old cells were unable to transfer all of their information over to the new cell due to oxygen and chi deficiency. Some of the defective oxygen- and chi-starved new cells may affect the part of the body that they represent – perhaps by preventing that part from working properly – and also affect the ageing process within the body. This could place the affected part of the body under stress and could be the cause of many of the diseases that are prevalent in the world today.

When we breathe correctly, all of the vital organs in the body will operate well within the capacity that they were designed for. This will ensure that all of our vital organs give us good service right up to the time of our departure from this world.

So how do we breathe correctly?

# Correct Breathing

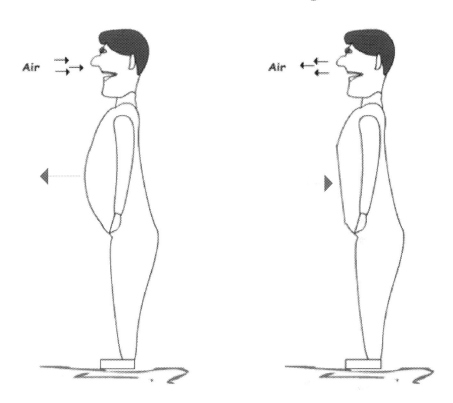

In the above diagram, you can see that when breathing correctly, one is breathing in through the nose and out through the nose. This is very important, especially when one is inhaling. The nose has the ability to control the temperature of the incoming breath so as to ensure that the air entering the lungs is at the right temperature. This will prevent the lungs from feeling any stress that may be caused by incoming cold air.

The nose is also able to filter incoming air by way of small hairs inside the nostrils. This filter will prevent any small particles from being sucked into the lungs while inhaling. If you breathe in through your mouth, there is no protection in place to stop particles from being sucked straight into the lungs. In winter, inhaling through the mouth introduces cold air straight into the lungs, and this can cause sharp pains in the chest, especially if one is hurrying. This is all extra stress that can trigger unexpected health problems.

The diagram also indicates the use of the diaphragm muscle when breathing. You can see that the stomach will expand outwards when you inhale and sink inwards when you exhale. When you are breathing this way, the shoulders do not move at all, and there is only a small movement in the chest. Diaphragmatic breathing ensures that the lungs will be fully inflated when inhaling, and when exhaling, they will be totally empty of all unwanted gases. This will reduce the possibility of stale gases remaining in the bottom of the lungs to cause respiratory problems in the future.

I have mentioned previously that correct breathing is best. So what other benefit would you expect to gain by changing the way you breathe, and would it be worth the hassle of changing anyway? It is true that many people who breathe using the shallow breathing method can live to a ripe old age, but it is *how* they live that is important, not *how long*. How often while walking along the street do you come across an old friend who you haven't seen for a while, and he or she says, "I feel fantastic! It is great to be alive. I know I'm 60, but I feel 21." Not very often, I suspect. But if you did, you could bet your bottom dollar that that individual is breathing correctly. Normally on meeting a friend, you have to stand there listening to tales of woe, closely followed by a depressing list of ailments.

It is quality and not quantity that matters. Why settle for eighty years of sickness, pain, and unhappiness when you could have seventy-five of the best years being fit, active, healthy, and happy? All you have to do is to change a few things in your life, and then you can live life to the full. Everybody has this opportunity; it is not only for a select few. Just follow the instructions in this book and any positive changes that you wish to implement will benefit your life immensely. Breathe correctly and you will be on the way to a healthy and happier way of life. Don't settle for anything less. Live life to the full.

# Chapter 3

# Relaxation

Total relaxation is the next step on the journey towards living life to the full. There are many interpretations of the word *relaxation*, but there is only one correct way to relax. To relax totally, you must begin with correct breathing. Correct breathing is the key to every other element involved with living life to the full. When you achieve the technique of correct breathing, then you will be more relaxed within.

Many people misunderstand the whole concept of relaxation. Relaxation is generally perceived as resting and not doing anything at all, but that is not relaxation. To many people, relaxation is sitting on the sofa with a glass of wine and watching the television. To others, it is walking on the beach or in the countryside. Still others find reading a good book to be relaxing. *True* relaxation isn't any of these things. Those of you who want to be in a truly relaxed state will have to work hard to achieve it. The hard work will start by correcting your breathing, as described in Chapter 2.

There are many people who struggle with their ego; this may apply to you, but you may not be aware that you have a problem. When someone has an egocentric manner, their only concern is for their own self-image. If they have a superiority complex that they inflict upon others, there is usually a stress-related problem within the mind that needs to be addressed.

Look at yourself and ask just one question: *Do I always fight to be right or can I let it go?* Egocentric people will always find themselves in the firing line of others, just waiting to be shot down from the elevated heights where they have placed themselves. Unfortunately, they leave themselves wide open. When someone is in a situation such as this, the stress placed upon that person will prevent him or her from being truly relaxed, and this will slow down or stop any personal progress. If you are suffering from stress in any part of the body, it will be impossible for you to be truly relaxed – and impossible to live life to the full.

Even if you achieve the other elements needed to live life to the full, it will not matter. If you have any stress in your body at all, you cannot be relaxed, and you will not be living your life to the full. You should work on getting rid of your ego so that you do not feel that you have anything to prove. You will be more content within yourself and one step closer to living life to the full.

While walking along the high street in any town or city with your mind open and your senses receptive, you may feel a background tension in the air. When I first observed this, it was as if at any moment something – I didn't know what – was going to explode. At first, I didn't understand what it was that I was actually sensing. During this time, I was teaching t'ai chi and qigong and helping my students to work with, and use, energy (chi). I was also a healer, using energy to help and to promote healing within others. I had a daily training regime then as I still have today, and the more I trained and promoted energy within myself, the more receptive I became to the things going on around me. My senses were sharper, and I was becoming more sensitive to vibrational frequencies.

When I started to become sensitive to the tensions around me, I realised that they were coming from other people. The tension was being emitted from people as they went about their normal daily business along the high street. I started to look into this phenomenon more closely, and I realised that almost all the people in the high street of my town had some form of stress, and they were carrying it around as if it was normal. I was shocked to see that stress affected so many people and they were not even aware of it. It was especially interesting to me as I didn't feel that I was being affected by stress myself.

One of the symptoms of stress within the body is raised shoulders. When the shoulders are raised whilst either walking or standing still, there will be tension in this and other areas. The chi inside the body, in this situation, will be raised higher than it should be. This means that when moving around, you are carrying the weight of your whole body with your shoulders. This is not only uncomfortable but can cause unnecessary pain from the resulting tension in the neck and shoulder muscles. This area may constantly ache because of the continual strain from holding up the body. This may also be the source of frequent back pain. By placing persistent stress on your shoulders, you run the risk of developing tension headaches and even migraine.

Another drawback to having your shoulders carry or hold up your body is the physical effort being used to do it. It is no wonder that the most common complaint people have with their life is that they are always tired. The solution for this is simple: develop the art of true relaxation and then let the ground take the strain, not your shoulders. Let's take a look at how we can develop true and lasting relaxation throughout the body.

The first thing that needs to be addressed, and I have said this many times before, is correct breathing. There is no point in even trying to relax if you aren't breathing correctly. Breathing, when done correctly, will bring vitality into the body and enhance life. When a person is relaxed, there is no tiredness or lethargy in their body at all. The body cannot have vitality and tiredness at the same time – these are complete opposites. Relaxation is not just flopping down on the sofa; when there is true relaxation, the body is still full of vitality. Relaxation is an invigorating experience. It is not something that one does to combat tiredness. Breathing correctly will give the body vitality, and then relaxation will bring to it that refreshing, calming, feel-good factor that makes life worth living.

To begin the relaxation process, you must be aware of the internal energy of your body. This energy is called *chi* or life-force energy; it is the same energy that is associated with t'ai chi and qigong. The name of this energy varies from country to country. For example, in Japan it is called *ki*, in India it is called *prana*, and in China it is call *qi*. Regardless of the name applied to it, the meaning is always the same. It is the life-force energy inside of the body that gives us life. There is only one internal energy in our body, and in this book I will call it chi.

When you lower the chi in your body (this is called sinking), you will notice a comforting feeling of warmth or coolness going through the body, as if the body is adjusting itself to the right temperature. There will also be a feeling of extra weight being applied to the feet, as if they were being pushed harder into the ground. When someone starts to perform the procedure of sinking, the weight that is being lifted by the shoulders will be transferred down into the feet and then into the ground – hence the saying "let the ground take the strain". When you begin to learn how to lower the chi in your body, the operation of sinking will immediately start the relaxation process.

How is it possible to lower the chi in the body? Energy follows thought, so if a person wanted to move chi around the body, then all he or she would have to do is think it there. To move chi into the feet, think of the feet. To move chi into the hands, think of the hands. It is as simple as that. Learning to feel and use chi is important, as it is a useful element to have if you are striving to live your life to the full. When you can work with and understand chi, you will be another step closer to true relaxation.

Chi is used for a number of things. Chi can help the mind and body relax when we work with it internally, thereby reducing stress. When we are able to reduce our stress levels, the mind and body perform much better and benefit greatly from the relaxation that occurs when stress is reduced. The body has an innate intelligence which uses chi to heal itself. There is no reason for anyone to become ill, as the body is designed to self-heal. It is able to perform its self-healing abilities around the clock all day every day for the whole of its life.

The body is constantly under attack from all kinds of diseases and would not be able to sustain life for very long without the ability to heal itself. So why then do we still become ill?

The answer is glaringly obvious, and yet so few people know about it. I think that the government and health authorities could benefit by working together to look for alternative ways of keeping the population healthy instead of bleating about how little money they have. Researching the possibility that the human body can actually heal itself would be an excellent starting point.

Once self-healing has been established as a fact, researchers can focus on why people are still becoming ill and dying, even though the body has the ability to self-heal. They might want to consider taking a look at why at least three quarters of the population of the UK are feeling unwell most of the time. Many of these people are on medication for much of their lives.

It is obvious why so many of us are ill. It is a lifestyle problem. The way we are living is killing us. Many people look to their peers for guidance with regard to how life should be lived. Yet the very leaders who are looked upon for guidance and leadership are failing the people they are leading. All aspects of living in our society have been spinning out of control for some time now. There is no guidance, there is no leadership, and the fundamental reason for this is that our peers and leaders have not been taught these lessons themselves. They are also influenced by the large corporations to keep things as they are, and people are suffering because of this.

We are eating too much of the wrong foods. Many foods on offer to people these days are processed foods that lack the vitamins and minerals the body needs to be healthy. When the body is deficient of the vitamins and minerals it needs, the immune system becomes weakened and leaves the body open to illness. Would responsible leaders allow this to happen if they were aware that it was happening? Would responsible leaders allow it to continue to happen if they were truly responsible leaders?

When there is a lack of vitamins or a lack of anything that the body needs to function properly, that lack will produce stress within the body, and then it will be impossible for the body to have true relaxation. Without the means to relax, the natural flow of energy (chi) will be impeded, thereby keeping the internal organs from functioning properly. To stay healthy and allow the body to self-heal, we must replenish its supply of chi daily. One of the ways to do this is by eating fresh food. All fresh natural food contains chi; processed foods do not.

I know that processed foods are convenient to prepare, and they can taste very nice, but many processed foods are laced with additives to make them taste good. These additives can also be addictive, so that the people who eat them will want to go out and buy them again at their next shopping trip. Isn't that sneaky? There is very little nourishment in most processed foods, which is why an hour or so after eating this type of food, you will feel hunger pangs start up again. The body still feels empty and is letting you know that it hasn't received the goodness it needs from the last meal you ate. I will talk more about nutrition and the affect of food on the body in another chapter.

Do you want to be healthy, or would you prefer to stay stressed and ill? The leaders of this country do not seem to be bothered either way. There is a definite correlation between relaxation and health. Chi will circulate around the body more freely when the body is relaxed; and when the body is relaxed, it is stress-free and healthier. Having a healthy relaxed body and mind will help you to live life to the full and to fill the space you occupy. This will help you grow as a person and progress to greater things.

## Meditation

Many people believe that to meditate, you have to be relaxed, but this is not so. You do not have to relax to meditate, but meditation does promote relaxation. When you practise meditation, the body and mind are definitely relaxed, although when the meditation is over the relaxation will probably stop too.

If practised regularly, meditation will calm your mind and help you to stay focused on the thoughts at hand. However, any benefit that you get from practising meditation will stop if you stop practising meditation. You cannot store up whatever benefits are received from meditation. If you don't do it, it doesn't work.

When meditation is practised regularly over a period of years, a definite change can be seen within the mind and body. This change affects the way you think, which in turn changes the way you perceive life. These changes affect the sensitivity of the mind, which will by now have become a little more refined. Occurrences that seemed normal before will now seem very coarse or even painful to the senses. This is not to say that the source of this coarseness is inferior; it just means that the mind is now more perceptive.

There are many techniques that can be used to help us when learning to meditate. At the beginning stage of learning meditation, most of the techniques are based on focus. Focusing the mind will help to bring it under your control and will also help to eliminate some of the unwanted thoughts that are constantly bombarding you.

When starting the meditation process, you should be sitting comfortably. It doesn't matter whether you're sitting cross-legged on the floor or sitting on a chair – being comfortable is the most important thing. When you are comfortable and ready to start meditating, your mind and body should be quiet. I mentioned in a previous chapter that breathing is the key to relaxation, so to begin the meditation, we shall do a breathing exercise.

While sitting, place your hands one on top of the other with the palms facing up. Breathe normally in through your nose and then out slowly through your mouth. The out breath should be at least five seconds long. As the breath leaves your mouth, your body and mind will start to become quiet. Repeat this exercise three times; try to breathe by using the diaphragm muscle mentioned earlier in this book. If there is any difficulty trying to quiet your mind, repeat the breathing exercise again.

Your body should now be receptive enough to start, so let us move on to the focusing part of meditation. The technique that I want to use in this book is a simple one that is ideal for those who are beginners but will also be appropriate for long-term practitioners of meditation. Let us focus on the lower dantian. The lower dantian lies about $1\frac{1}{2}$ to 2 inches below the navel and about 1 inch behind the navel. It is known as the sea or ocean of chi and holds many mysteries. I will be writing more about the dantians in a future chapter.

To focus on the lower dantian, just think of that area, but do not think of it on the surface of the body; think of it inside – 1 inch inside of the skin. When learning new skills, difficulties can often arise, and meditation is no exception. When placing your attention on the lower dantian, do not expect to see or feel anything straight away. The purpose of focusing on this area is to help you learn how to calm down the body and quiet the mind.

At first, with most beginners to meditation, there will be a constant battle with random thoughts barging their way into the mind. As these thoughts emerge, acknowledge that they are there and then let them drift away. Do not get angry or impatient with yourself for not being able to stop them. Frustration will only take you further away from your goal. After a while – and this depends on the individual – this interruption will slowly start to die away. As this happens, there will be, from time to time, quiet moments in the mind. When these moments become noticeable, use them to become aware of the lower dantian.

When you have learned the basic technique of meditation, it is best to practise it every day. I know that this may seem a little extreme, as most activities that people engage in are only done once or twice a week. I bet that you are also wondering where on earth you are going to find the time to commit to this daily regime. When you first start practising meditation, you only need to commit yourself to ten minutes a day; if you are not able to give ten minutes out of twenty-four hours, then perhaps meditation is not for you.

If there is no problem with this commitment, then after two weeks of practice at ten minutes each day, increase the practice time to fifteen minutes. Thereafter, increase the time a little more every few weeks, or when you feel ready to, until you eventually reach a meditation time of thirty minutes. Once you settle down with the practice of meditation, you will eventually want to meditate for longer periods of time. When this point is reached, you will already have noticed that meditation is changing your life, and then you will start to realise that the practice of meditation is for life.

When practised every day, meditation will help you to develop a strong mind. It will give you the ability to handle stressful situations as they arise. The breathing exercise that was used to start the meditation can be used in other situations also. As an example: If you are going for a job interview or perhaps taking a driving test, using this breathing exercise beforehand will help to calm your body and mind by relieving the anxiety. Meditation is a valuable tool to have, it will keep your mind sharp, help you to become more spiritually aware, and also give you a better perspective on your surroundings and the people who live in them.

The practice of meditation will have a profound effect on your life by changing previously held perceptions of the world outside. This, in time, will provide a greater insight into your own values and wisdom. By practising meditation every day and combining it with the other components mentioned previously, you will have a better chance to fill the space you occupy and live life to the full.

## Contemplation

I have found that, through the practice of meditation over a period of many years, my mind and the way that I think have changed considerably. I know that what I think about today is very different from what I thought about ten years ago. My values have changed, and things that were important to me in my life then have lost their importance. I am not talking about the day-to-day fads and fancies we all have as we go through life. The changes that I experienced were as a direct result of practising meditation – which, in turn, led me to develop the art of contemplation.

The changes made to the mind through the practise of meditation start to take place when the mind is able to maintain focus for long periods. This will enable you to contemplate something that requires your complete attention. Contemplation is a powerful tool to have in the toolbox of life. Develop the power of contemplation by learning and practising the art of patience. Patience is essential if you want to maintain focus during your meditational practice, and this will lead you to the development of contemplation. Contemplation is the ability to maintain a single thought whilst keeping all random thoughts at bay.

When you are able to hold a single thought for a period of time, you can then expand that thought by choosing a subject of interest which can be dissected by the mind and analysed from every aspect. This description may sound very clinical, but when it is applied to your own life and interests, it can become extremely useful.

There are many situations where contemplation can help you. For instance, if there is a difficult problem that needs to be solved, applying focus to the situation allows you to look at the problem at hand from every aspect without being distracted either by random thoughts or the encroachment of stray sounds that are within earshot. When the focus is total, the problem will be solved sooner than you would have thought possible. By applying contemplative thought to any situation that needs the application of a sharp mind – which is basically every situation – you can eliminate the possibility of any stress or anxiety occurring beforehand. Although contemplation is not one of the main components needed to live life to the full, it is certainly a useful ally when confronting problems from which stress and anxiety can arise.

## Key points

Let us take a look back at what we have covered so far. Living life to the full means different things to different people, but the following elements are necessary for all:

- **Correct breathing** is the first main component needed to live life to the full. Breathing is a natural and automatic process. When you breathe by using the diaphragm, you are breathing correctly, and this will ensure that the lungs receive the right amount of oxygen. Inhaling through the nose also ensures that when air fills the lungs, it will be at the right temperature and suitably filtered.
- **Relaxation** is the second main component needed to live life to the full. The key to relaxation is correct breathing. True relaxation will help to relieve stress both internally and externally. Recognise your chi (internal energy). Once you are aware of your chi, by lowering it inside your body, you help your body begin to relax. Once this happens, your stress level will decrease and your relaxation level will increase. To maintain a relaxed mental state, do not gossip, curb all egotistical thoughts, and do not place yourself in a position where you can easily be toppled from the pedestal that you have put yourself on. Get rid of your ego.
- **Health** is the third main component needed to live life to the full, and the first two components give you a good

start. Take on the responsibility for your own health; do not rely on others to make you better when you are ill. Learn to live life to the full and you will not become ill. Rid your body and mind of stress and illness will disappear. Practice meditation and contemplation to keep stress levels down. Your body has the ability to heal itself, so do not overburden it by eating the wrong food, doing the wrong exercise, or thinking the wrong thoughts. These things produce stress and will make you ill.

# Chapter 4

# Exercise

Over the past twenty to thirty years, there have been huge changes within the working practice of people throughout Europe, America, and other industrially advanced areas. This is due mainly to the advancement of technology. A large proportion of the workforce has been made redundant. They have been forced to exchange their manual jobs for office-based employment because skilled manual work has been automated and is performed by computerised machines. This has affected the amount of exercise manual workers do now that they have been moved from a physical job to a job that requires them to sit at a desk for most of the day. To maintain a healthy mind and body, it is crucial for those who are relatively inactive throughout their working day to exercise regularly.

In many countries of the Western world, the collective health and fitness levels of the population have deteriorated considerably, and the consumption of unhealthy processed food has increased. This makes it all the more important for everybody to exercise daily. Exercise can be practised at any time of day, but for a lot of people, weekdays are difficult, especially for those who go to work. For these individuals, exercise should be done either in the morning before eating breakfast or after work before the evening meal. Exercising on the weekend is ideal, as there is probably more free time available, and most people are more relaxed during this period. I do recommend, though, that everybody do some exercise every day.

Let's take a look at a typical working day. Most people wake up to the sound of an alarm clock. Their nerves jangled, they roll out of bed and go through the morning ablutions. They have their first cup of tea or coffee of the day, but they miss breakfast because time is tight. They jump in the car and start the rush hour trek to work.

While working through the morning, they will consume a few more cups of tea or coffee and maybe eat a mid-morning snack bar. At lunchtime, they will have a working lunch, maybe a sandwich eaten at their desk. While working through the afternoon, they will consume more coffee and perhaps a cake or a bag of crisps. After working half an hour of unpaid overtime, they will get back into the car to join the evening rush hour and make their way back home. The evening meal will probably be eaten in front of the TV with a couple more cups of tea or coffee – or perhaps a beer or a couple of glasses of wine. Then it is time for bed.

Apart from the short walks to the coffee machine and a couple of trips to the loo, it doesn't seem to me that there was very much exercise going on there at all. Exercise is much like food; there are good exercises and bad exercises, but the *correct* exercise is best. Any exercise in moderation is better than no exercise, so let us take a look at the difference between good and bad exercises to see what effects they have on the body.

To start with, I must say that whatever exercise is practised, whether it is the right kind of exercise or the wrong kind, if it is performed to excess then be prepared for damage to the body. The damage could be something minor like a sprained ligament or a pulled muscle or tendon; though extremely painful at the time, such minor injuries will repair themselves within a week or two. Then there are the more serious types of injury mainly caused by excessive practice that produces wear and tear on the body over a period of years. Excessive exercise can lead to worn out joints, irreversible muscle damage, and internal organ damage to your body.

Then there are the kinds of exercise where you are constantly pushing yourself to the limit each time you practice. With this type of training, it is possible to incur injuries such as snapped Achilles tendons and badly torn leg, arm, or back muscles. Injuries like these could put you out of action for months, but when the severity of the damage is more serious, you could easily be laid up for a year or more. With this excessive kind of exercising, surgery may be required to repair damage to the body. If the damage cannot be repaired, the individual may be unable to exercise again, and also experience restricted freedom of movement for the rest of his or her life. Being disabled in this way is a frightening prospect for those who are otherwise healthy and mentally active but who have unfortunately travelled down the path of extremism.

When choosing a fitness regime, think carefully about what is right for you and what you hope to achieve by practising the type of exercise you have chosen. If you are suffering joint problems – for example, arthritis – athletic exercises such as running, jumping, rock climbing, and bobsleigh riding will probably not be for you.

Many people take up running as a means of keeping themselves fit. It seems to be trendy and the "in thing" to do nowadays. People who take up running probably get their inspiration from watching events like the Olympic Games and many other major events that are held worldwide. If your goal is staying fit and healthy, I am sorry to say that running is the wrong kind of exercise. I am not saying that running, when done in moderation, will not contribute to the overall fitness of the body, but if it is the only exercise practised on a daily basis, the body will slowly wear out and may experience muscle and joint pain in later life. In extreme cases, there is the potential for a permanent disability. This type of exercise is extreme and will not help you to achieve a life that is lived to the full.

Just think for one moment: Why has the body been given the ability to run? Running is a fight-or-flight response. If you do not want to stay and fight, moving out of the way quickly is the next best thing, hence the ability to run. The body is not designed to run all of the time. Running is only meant to be done occasionally in short bursts when it is necessary, for example, running after an antelope in the bush in order to catch your evening meal, or running away from a bear who is hoping to make you his evening meal!

Running too often and for long distances places stress on many parts of the body. It is easy for the body to get used to and accept stress as a normal condition, but with persistent physical stress, there is a breaking point. When that point is reached, the damage done to the body may be permanent. I believe that running is therefore the wrong type of exercise to engage in. It is worth remembering that if there is any stress in the body at all, you will not be relaxed and therefore cannot be living life to the full.

When I think of how inventive our species has been throughout history, devising the many exercises that we are able to practice today to keep ourselves fit and healthy, I often wonder why we didn't take into account the issue of stress on the body. It would appear obvious that if people lift heavy weights above their head that far exceed their normal capability, performing this exercise comfortably without injury is impossible. Yet many people train their body to try to do just that. Why?

I believe it is their ego that compels them to seek out competition either against themselves or others. It is a ridiculous situation, as there is no real need for competition, especially when there is a risk of damaging the body. There is no need to compete against yourself or anyone else; you can never totally win anyway. Get rid of your ego. If you are competing, then you are not living life to the full. Competition in life will always ends in tears eventually, for all competitors.

If you push your body beyond its normal capability, no matter what form of exercise you practise, it will eventually become damaged and will cease to function properly. Would you really want spend the rest of your life in pain and discomfort, feeling miserable? Your body is a tool that is loaned to you for the purpose of living in this world. You are here for a short period only to learn the lessons that are needed for your own advancement. You are only here because this world has the right conditions to help you achieve this. You only have this one body for an allotted period of time, so if you abuse it by placing upon it unnecessary stress that will shorten its life, you will then be unable to complete the lessons. The consequence of a shortened life is the need to return here again to resume the learning of lessons that should have been learnt already. You will have to stay here until they are completed. For most people, this is not the best place in the universe to be, so why would you want to come back time and again when you shouldn't really need to?

While you are in this world, it is all about this body. Get rid of your ego and be sensible with your body. Give it the same respect you would give to your car. Treat it right by living life to the full. To do this, breathe correctly, be relaxed at all times, practise the correct exercise, and maintain the correct diet. This will help to remove any stress from your body so that it can last you right up to the point when you are ready to leave this world.

## Correct exercise

The correct kind of exercise is crucial to living your life to the full, so let's look at how we can adopt the practice of exercising correctly. We have previously looked at how easy it is to damage the body by practising incorrect exercise. It is time now to look at how easy it is to bring the body back to health and vitality. The exercises I am proposing will keep the body fit and healthy. They will also prevent disease and internal problems.

The exercises I am referring to have been around for thousands of years, but many people have never heard of them – or, if they have, they have made their own assumptions about what these are, based on gossip and hearsay. I am talking about qigong and t'ai chi. I would like to introduce you to these powerful Eastern arts by way of my own experience from the practice and teaching of them over the past seventeen years.

I will start by revealing how I damaged my body by practising the wrong kind of exercise. Before I took on the practice of t'ai chi and qigong, I spent twelve years practising and teaching Shotokan karate. I was an enthusiastic practitioner and teacher, attending three classes a week and spending the remainder of the week training at home. Karate is a hard sport that takes a lot out of the body. Because I took my karate training so seriously – training for long periods every day of the week – I never built into the training programme any period for recovery. In fact, recovery time was never mentioned by my instructors.

As a result of this non-stop training, the muscles around the joints of my hips and knees became damaged. The damage increased as I continued my training. Eventually, after about five years of suffering, I was forced to give up karate altogether. I realised some time later that it was my ego that kept me practising. Because I wouldn't let go, I suffered for longer than I should have. A short while after I stopped my karate training, a friend mentioned that I might get some benefit from joining a t'ai chi class. Although I had heard of t'ai chi, I had no clue as to what it actually was.

The practice of t'ai chi was a complete change from karate. Instead of the lightning fast and powerful technique of karate, t'ai chi was painfully slow. It took several months to get used to the change of speed when executing the movements, even though the movements were very similar. I practised t'ai chi in the same way that I practised karate, with great enthusiasm. I went to the class once a week, but I practised every day. After six months of training, I started to feel the benefit of practising t'ai chi. My mind and body started to slow down, and I was feeling more relaxed within myself. My thoughts were a little clearer, and there was a definite improvement in my hips and knees.

I carried on training every day and now attended two classes a week. I didn't have to worry about any recovery time, as with t'ai chi, there is nothing to recover from. I had been training continuously for around fifteen months and had made enough improvement to be offered by my instructor the chance of training to become an instructor myself, which I was pleased to accept.

As the months passed, the benefit I received from my t'ai chi training was quite marked. The damage to my hips and knees caused by karate had almost healed, and for the first time in over ten years my body didn't ache. My life had changed so much that my old self was unrecognisable. I was feeling extremely healthy. My thoughts were clear, and my body was the fittest it had been in a long time.

Throughout the years that I practised karate, I was taught that strength, speed, and power were all that mattered. My instructors did not say – and to be fair, they probably didn't know – that karate was probably not the best training method to use to achieve these things. Karate is an extreme sport that, for the dedicated, becomes a way of life. As with all sports, the competitions usually end in tears, and in many cases it is likely to cause more harm to the body than good. It is the wrong kind of exercise.

If you choose to practice t'ai chi, you will easily achieve strength, speed, and power. T'ai chi makes the body strong both internally and externally. Inner strength is equally as important, if not more so, than outer physical strength. T'ai chi will help the body react quickly, especially in a situation where there is a need for speed. This may sound strange because when practising t'ai chi, the movements are mainly slow, controlled, and coordinated, but the affect this has on the mind and body is to allow the reflex action to become faster.

The practice of t'ai chi will, with the advantage of inner strength, make it possible for the mind and body to go that extra mile when stamina is needed. When you empower your mind and body through t'ai chi, you can accomplish so much more in life. Practitioners of t'ai chi are able to attain that which would normally be out of reach, and this is due to the extra staying power they are able to achieve.

As we get older, we can lose confidence, especially if we have a fall. We may also sustain injuries because of a lack of judgement in our movement. When practising t'ai chi, our judgement remains intact because our mind stays sharp. With the regular practice of t'ai chi, we are less likely to have a fall because we are able to maintain and even improve our balance. This will help us to regain our confidence. Through the practice of t'ai chi, our normal level of confidence in later life is not only maintained but also grows when the fear of falling is alleviated. We look forward to a vast improvement in the general health and well-being of mind and body.

These are not just wild statements; there is plenty of documented proof available of the life improvement that the practice of t'ai chi can bring. I personally know three students who have benefited from practising t'ai chi. Each of these students was on medication for high blood pressure, and two of them had been on this medication for over ten years. Within a period of eighteen months of practising t'ai chi just once a week in the class and a couple of times a week at home, their blood pressure had fallen to such a level that their GP had to lower the dose of the medication. After further monitoring, they were taken off of the medication all together.

One of these three students, an older gentleman, also suffered from pain in both legs. He had to sit out and watch in some of the classes he attended, as the pain was too bad. Nevertheless, he would come to the class every week despite the pain. When he was finally taken off the blood pressure medication, the pain in his legs stopped, and he was able to complete every class he came to. The pain turned out to be one of the side effects of the medication he was on.

Drugs are, in many cases, a necessary remedy for helping to alleviate the symptoms of health problems we all seem to be susceptible to. But there are many other remedies that – whether out of lack of knowledge or lack of interest – are ignored completely by doctors, pharmaceutical companies, and the medical profession in general. Many of these remedies are extremely effective when used to treat illness, pain, and suffering, and they carry no side effect. There is very little research done outside of drug-related remedies, because that's where the money is. The suffering that is going on doesn't seem to matter; what seems to be more important is how much profit can be made.

T'ai chi and qigong hold a special importance with regard to health-related issues, but they are almost totally ignored by the mainstream medical profession. Doctors and researchers would be wise to take notice. Preventing illness from happening in the first place is the correct way to tackle many of the health problems that we are faced with today. Educating people to prevent illness is the way we should be going. The regular practise of t'ai chi and qigong is a step in the right direction that will promote the health and well-being of people of all nations. T'ai chi and qigong are the correct exercises to practice and are components that will help the people of every nation to live life to the full.

## Qigong

I have mentioned qigong a number of times in this chapter, and you may be wondering what exactly it is. I have been practising and teaching qigong now for a number of years, and I can only describe it as a breath of fresh air for the body and mind. Many moves in the t'ai chi form are constructed from moves practised in qigong. T'ai chi is probably 2,000 to 2,500 years old. Qigong dates back as far as 3,000 and possibly 5,000 years.

It is said that there are more than 90,000 different individual moves in qigong. As with t'ai chi, there are many different styles. Some of these moves are joined together to form a set, while others are practised individually and are just as powerful in their own right. When you start the practice of qigong for the first time, there are easy moves to perform which are Ideal for beginners. There are also intermediate techniques for when your body adjusts and becomes stronger and more flexible with regular practice, and then there are advanced techniques for when you have a few years of experience under your belt.

Qigong can be practised slowly or at a medium pace, or even fast, such as with kung fu and other martial arts techniques. Many of the moves in qigong are executed while standing in one position, while in other techniques, like t'ai chi, push hands, and kung fu, the moves are executed while travelling around.

As with t'ai chi, qigong originated in China but has recently become popular in many countries, although it is still little known in the UK. If you take the opportunity to join a qigong class, what should you expect? Well, if you stick at it and practice at home, then you should expect it to change your life. It will not increase the length of your life, as some practitioners and instructors would have you believe, but it will keep you extremely fit and really healthy right up until the day.

Let's talk about the positive benefit that practising qigong will bring you. For one thing, you will learn how to coordinate your breath with your movements. When you are able to achieve this, you will bring peace, balance, and harmony to both mind and body. Another benefit from this coordination is that chi will lower within you, promoting relaxation throughout the body.

When the body is relaxed, chi will flow more freely around it. So what does that mean? When chi is flowing around the body freely and smoothly, it is keeping the internal organs healthy. Chi is one of the requirements needed by all of the organs of the body to maintain good health and to stay happy and in good working order. When you are in a state of relaxation, there can be no stress present either in the mind or the body, so all-round health is maintained.

The goal, therefore, is to create a situation whereby your whole being is free from stress pretty much all of the time. This cannot help but change your life for the better, and as your life changes its course, the possibilities and opportunities presented to you may at first be difficult to comprehend, as they would have previously been beyond your reach.

As with t'ai chi, when practising qigong there will be gentle stretching. Whether you are working on a form or doing individual movements, your breathing must be coordinated with the general flow of the movement of your body, and your mind must be quiet but focused on what you are doing. Every action will be performed with total relaxation. The calming effect will be felt throughout every part of your body, but you will not be falling asleep; you will be working very hard.

The gentle stretching that happens with every movement when practising qigong will strengthen your tendons, muscles, and ligaments, making them stronger and more flexible without tearing them. Other sporting activities that people participate in to strengthen their muscles and tendons, have to be practised to the extreme to get this result. Practitioners of other sports tend to stretch too far, run too hard, and lift weights that are too heavy. They drive their body to extreme lengths by overstretching their tendons and ripping the tissues of their muscles to make them bigger, stronger, and more flexible in the shortest time possible.

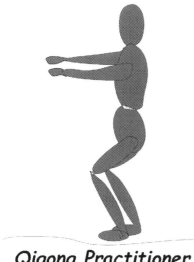

**Qigong Practitioner**

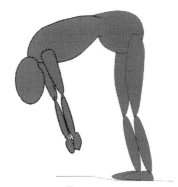

**Runner**

This illustration is a good example of correct exercise and incorrect exercise. No matter what the sport or exercise is, if the practitioners finish their activity and adopt a position where they are gasping for breath and looking like the figure on the right, this is the wrong exercise and is clearly causing a lot of stress to the body.

This type of extreme exercise places the body under a great deal of stress. If continued for long periods of time, it will eventually result in a breakdown of the area affected by the stress. One of the reasons that most top athletes retire from their sport in their early thirties is because their performance starts to decline. Their body begins to complain about the treatment that it has put up with over the years. Too much stress has affected the body, and it cannot perform to the same high standard any longer. In many cases, it has also sustained damaged beyond repair.

Qigong, when performed correctly, never places your body under so much stress that it will be damaged. When you practice qigong, your whole being is in a state of total relaxation. You cannot have stress and total relaxation in your body at the same time. Many people who practice qigong can do so well into their nineties and beyond. Because the organs, tendons, muscles, and mind are never placed under excessive stress, they are not affected detrimentally by the exercise being performed; they remain in perfect health and perfect working order, just as they were designed to be, throughout the whole of their life.

You can create a body and mind that will be healthy, strong, flexible, and in excellent working order – and remain so for a lifetime. This can be achieved easily with the regular practice of qigong and t'ai chi. I cannot place too much emphasis on the practice of these two activities, and I will now explain a little more about other benefits that will be gained when you move on beyond the beginner's stage.

Qigong is a healing art. When you expand your practice of qigong beyond the needs of your physical self, a new paradigm will be unveiled. This will be the perception of internal energy. Internal energy is known in the Far Eastern countries as chi, and as explained earlier in this book, chi is the power that the body uses to heal itself. There are many people who profess to be healers of one kind or another. They travel around in many guises. Some have expensive clinics, and they purport to heal the sick and injured. Many charge large fees for this service.

No one can heal anyone else. It is not possible. The service that a so-called healer provides (incidentally, I am one myself) is not to heal others but to promote the start of the healing process by making the body aware that there is something wrong within it. A healer can provide the kick-start needed by projecting energy into the affected area of the body. The body being treated will then recognise what is happening and respond by using its own energy to heal itself.

Why would a sick or injured body not be aware that it has a problem? Just take a look at that way people are living in our society. The lifestyle that many people lead will always encourage stress, either physical or mental. Stress affects the whole body, wearing it down until the immune system becomes very low and ineffective and the circulation of chi within the body slows down or becomes blocked. This will make self-healing unlikely if problems arise.

The body replenishes its chi supply twenty-four hours a day when we eat, drink, and breathe, and also by attraction. When you have a high level of stress, the replenishment of chi is much slower. If you eat foods or drink drinks that have little or no chi in them, and you are also breathing incorrectly, there will be very little replenishment. If chi is unable to flow around the body freely and smoothly, the immediate health of the body is in question. The long-term prospects for a person in this condition are not good.

A person with stress cannot be relaxed, and chi will not be attracted into the body while it has a stress problem. Therefore, the immune system will remain weak. It is a catch-22 situation that can only be resolved by helping your mind and body return to the position of being naturally relaxed. The solution to this problem is to eliminate stress. This can be easily achieved by incorporating into your life the regular practice of t'ai chi, qigong, or meditation. When we include either or all of these practises as a regular part of our lifestyle, we bring balance back into our life. With a higher level of energy/chi within the body, the effectiveness of the body's ability to heal itself will increase immensely.

If qigong is practised regularly, the energy or chi levels within the body will always be higher. Because the body will be naturally relaxed, it will always be able to replenish its energy supply. Chi will always be flowing freely and smoothly around it to keep it healthy and in good working order. As you become more aware of internal energy and how it works within the body, with practice, you can direct chi to areas within your body that are affected by disease or damage and help your body heal itself more easily and more effectively.

With regular practice of qigong, your vibrational frequency will increase, especially if your practice is focused on both the internal energy aspect of qigong (*neidan*) and the physical external elements (*waidan*) together. You may also find that your spiritual awareness will increase. This does not mean that you will have an insatiable urge to rush out and join a religious order. You will just be more aware of your purpose here on earth, and it will generally broaden your outlook on life. You will frequently have feelings of elation the more you work with energy, especially when doing so within your meditation practice. T'ai chi and qigong are the right kind of exercises. Only good can come out of these practises: health improvement, clarity within your mind, and a higher sense of self-worth.

There is a style of qigong that is practised by many experienced qigong practitioners that I haven't mentioned in this chapter yet. This style of qigong would seem to be a contradiction of everything I have said about qigong so far. It is called *hard qigong*. The type of qigong I have previously written about is referred to as *soft qigon*g. Halfway between these two is *soft hard qigong.*

Hard qigong is best practised by someone who already has some experience of t'ai chi or soft qigong and is aware of how chi works within the body. Before taking on the practice of hard qigong, it is wise to make sure that you are physically fit and have no injuries or medical conditions, especially if you are on medication for high blood pressure or if you have heart-related problems, muscle damage, or joint problems like arthritis. It is wise to find an experienced instructor to teach you hard qigong and guide you carefully. If you are not sure about your health, ask your doctor first whether you are fit enough to train.

It is better to start practising hard qigong when you are young. I came to the practice fairly late in life, but it suited me after the years of t'ai chi, soft qigong, and meditation training I had undergone. Although I am older now, I still practice hard qigong, but I now mix my hard qigong practice with soft qigong, soft hard qigong, and t'ai chi. There are many benefits to be gained from practising hard qigong. Hard qigong training will increase your muscle strength throughout your body without building muscle bulk. This kind of training will keep you very fit and fast.

Many practitioners of the martial arts use hard qigong within their training regime, as it helps to protect them from serious injury in combat. Every part of the body becomes extremely strong and can take immense punishment before serious injury occurs. Chi can be directed to the area of impact to prevent injury not just when fighting but anytime your body is active and can become injured. The body literally becomes as strong as iron.

Because of the nature of hard qigong training, your general health will improve as your internal organs become stronger. They will be able to handle the workload they have to endure throughout their life more easily and so are less likely to break down. It is also claimed that hard qigong increases longevity, but nobody can live beyond his or her allotted lifespan. T'ai chi, qigong, and meditation are all tools you can use to help you to live life to the full.

## Key points

Let's take another look at some important points from this chapter:

- **Incorrect exercise**, if practised to excess, can cause severe stress on the parts of the body used, so much so that recovery time will be needed before the exercise can be practised again. Long-term practice of these types of exercise could affect the performance of the body in later life and may severely damage it beyond repair, leaving the practitioner partially or even totally disabled. It is a fallacy to believe that *all* exercise is good for you. There is no need to compete with yourself or with anyone else. This world is not merely competitive; it also has a creative side, and when you compete you will never really win. Lose the ego and concentrate on creative opportunities. They will be much more rewarding.
- **Correct exercise** generates no stress on the body or mind but still produces a strong, flexible, and healthy

body with a mind that has greater clarity of thought, prolonged concentration, and greater flexibility. T'ai chi and qigong fit these criteria. With regular practice, they will give the practitioner all of the above attributes and bring about change that is certain to be for the better. When your body is fit, strong, and flexible, and stress is eliminated from the mind and body, you can start living life to the full.

· Many people use this world as a holiday resort and think that we are here just for a good time. This world is actually a place where we are able to learn and experience the lessons that have been set for us and which are our purpose for being here. The time for a holiday is when the learning has finished and we leave this world

# Chapter 5

# **Food**

Isn't food great? You could eat it all day long – and many people do. Did you know that obesity is the fastest-growing medical condition in the UK, Europe, and America? People are eating themselves into an early grave. I am now going to cover various ways that you can change this without going on any of these so-called wonder diets. I am not saying that you won't have to modify your eating habits. What I am going to suggest is that you should try *correct* eating and drinking.

Let's start with some very basic suggestions. When you start to eat the right kind of food – that is, food that contains the goodness that your body needs to maintain itself – you will first have to get the bad stuff – such as toxins – out of your cells in order to get the good stuff – vitamins, minerals, and other essentials – in. This process is called *detoxification*. We all need to detoxify.

There are many ways to detoxify your body. The method I would recommend is the one that I use myself. It's cheap and easy to do, and it is very effective It starts with drinking water before doing anything else when you wake up in the morning. Drink one, or if you can manage it, two or more glasses of water every day. When you begin your day in this way, you will start the process of moving the toxins out of your body through the bowels, leaving the cells clean, fresh, and ready to take in the good stuff.

There is no point in changing your diet to the right kind of food and drink without detoxifying. The toxins you have already taken into your body by eating and drinking manufactured food and drink and ingesting chemically sprayed fresh food will remain inside your body, possibly causing more problems to your health and well-being when you start to eat and drink healthily. They need to be removed. If you are not ill, there is no need to spend a lot of money having yourself flushed out with whatever technique is in fashion at the moment. Remove the toxins from your body gradually by drinking water at the beginning of your day before you do anything else.

When you drink water in this way, you flush out your system, and you will feel healthier and more vibrant when your day begins. You may also notice, if you are overweight, that your weight drops naturally as you bring your body back into balance.

Another tool you might like to try is lemon water. Squeeze the juice of half an unwaxed lemon into a glass and then top up with water. Lemon is a good body cleanser. Most mornings, I drink a glass of water followed by a glass of lemon water before I get going.

It is widely said that "You are what you eat." If you eat rubbish, you will not feel as vibrant or as healthy as you might otherwise do. So what makes a food source rubbish? This type of food is wide ranging is generally described as junk food, meaning food that has little or no goodness in it. When it is consumed, the body receives very little nutrition, and you feel as though you could eat it all again because of the appetite and flavour-enhancing chemicals that are added to the food when it is processed. In effect, it is a waste of time eating it in the first place. It goes in one end and comes out the other, leaving very little value or benefit to the body that has consumed it. In most cases, it leaves behind whatever toxic chemical substances it contains within the cell structure of your body, along with any excess fats and sugars, which the body stores as fat. I am, of course, referring here to foods that are processed, sprayed with chemicals, or genetically modified.

## Processed foods

Some processed foods have been manufactured totally from beginning to end, while others were at one time fresh and nutritious but have had the goodness removed from them, either in the preparation or the processing stage. I am also referring here to foods that were alive and kicking at one time but have been slaughtered, worked on, and stuffed into a pie, pudding, tin, or packet. You just don't know what parts of the animal have been used to fill out these products. Knowing how much a businessman enjoys making money, you can bet your life that they are not going to be filled out with the most expensive cuts of meat, are they?

Totally manufactured foods start their life in a laboratory rather than from the land, sea, or air. They are made by combining various chemical ingredients. Many of these ingredients are harmless when eaten – but some, when eaten in large quantities, may actually poison your body. Chemical ingredients such as sugar substitutes are put into products purposely because of their addictive qualities. Some are derived from land-based crops such as soya, wheat, or corn. Other chemical additives in the processing operation are deemed to be harmless, but many have not yet stood the test of time.

The end result of all this manufacturing is a noxious chemical soup that is then combined with more chemicals to hold it together, and still more chemicals to give it flavour and colour to make it aesthetically pleasing. When the product is finished and packaged, it may look and taste wonderful, but will probably contain little actual nutrition. Most importantly, it will not contain any chi.

## Fresh foods

Fruits, vegetables, nuts, and seeds have such a diverse range of variety and colour and cover such a broad spectrum of vitamin, mineral, and fatty acid content that it is possible to get everything that the body needs in the way of nutritional requirement from them without eating meat or fish and without taking any supplements. However, unfortunately, there is bad news here too. Most of the fruits and vegetables that are available for us to buy these days have been sprayed with chemicals while they are either in the ground or hanging from a tree.

Fresh produce is sprayed with insecticides, herbicides, and fungicides. It doesn't matter how fresh the marketing says these items are when you buy them, they are still coated with chemicals. Just a simple rinse under the tap may not be enough to remove it. The residue from chemical sprays on our food can cause people to develop allergic reactions, chemical intolerance, stomach complaints, nausea, and unexplained headaches, to name just a few side effects.

There is a solution for this: buy organic fruits, vegetables, nuts, and seeds. In most cases, organic products will be a few pence dearer, but they are a healthier option and well worth paying the extra. Eating organic will help to prevent chemical toxins from being ingested and building up inside the cells of your body.

## Genetically modified (GM) foods

Foods that have had their DNA altered in a laboratory are said to be genetically modified. So what does that actually mean? Through the advancement and understanding of genetics, scientists can now engineer the DNA structure of plants and animals. This means that they can alter the genes of any plant or animal by adding or taking away genetic material. Genetic material that has been extracted from another species of plant or animal will alter the genetic makeup of the plant or animal that has had this material placed in its DNA. This will make the altered plant or animal behave or appear different from how it would normally be.

Why would anyone want to do this? Evidently, it is being done to save millions of lives in the Third World of people dying from starvation. In reality, though, there *is* no Third World – there is only *one* world, and we all live on it together. Why not send starving people normal unaltered food instead of using them as laboratory rats?

The real reason large multinational companies are going to all the trouble of producing GM foods is not because saving the lives of poor and underprivileged people is the number-one concern on their agenda; it is all to do with money and power. When the mistakes and problems have been ironed out of the genetically altered food, it will be at the expense and the health of the poorer people of this world. Who will come out on top? The companies who manufacture GM food, of course. They can now sell this food to the governments of the poorer countries, thereby making themselves even richer and more powerful than they already are.

What kinds of alterations are made to the genes of plants and animals? In one example, genes are taken from a drought-tolerant plant and added to a plant that cannot survive in dry conditions, thereby turning it into a plant that can tolerate dryer desert-like conditions. This looks like a good idea at first glance – getting crops to grow in the desert – but what of the consequences of this action? No one knows the long-term effect modified food will have on the people who eat it, and no one knows the long-term effect this will have on the environment where these crops are planted.

Another common modification is to engineer the seeds of crops that are vulnerable to insect attacks to contain a built-in pesticide. Have the seed producers considered the possibility that insects and other pests that are continually exposed to this kind of deterrent may become resistant to these pesticides in a relatively short space of time? And what is the effect on humans? It will no longer be possible to wash pesticides off of food because the pesticide will now be a part of the food's genetic structure. We will have no choice but to consume it. Would you get a can of fly killer and spray it in your mouth? I'll leave you to think about that one.

The alterations that geneticists can make to plants, animals, or for that matter, any living thing seem to be as diverse as their imagination. I have only covered a few points about GM foods here to bring to your attention this matter and pose the question: Is it possible that GM foods will have an effect on whether or not you will be able to live your life to the full?

We have looked at the downside of GM food, and there are many more that will have to be sorted out before the benefits, if any, become obvious. But what about the *good* side of this science? Should we, as a people, go down the route of genetic alteration and manufacturing? Is it morally right to do so? This kind of work is in its infancy, but like all scientific development work of importance, the benefits that genetic engineering will bring to mankind in the future will be invaluable, and will play a significant part in the evolution of the human race. There will always be stumbling blocks along the way; but it is my belief that this work should carry on and as we continue to develop as human beings, and in the passage of time, we will eventually become the creators of man and all things, and this will not be too far into the future. We shall eventually emulate our forebears just as we and all things here have been created.

## Tobacco and alcohol

They say "You are what you eat" and "As you think, so you are." The brain is our most powerful organ. It is responsible for everything we do, say, think, and feel. Knowing this, it is reasonable to assume that everyone would be pretty keen to look after it. However, this statement couldn't be further from the truth. We abuse our brain in the same way that we abuse the rest of our body.

The brain comes under immense stress when we smoke either normal cigarettes or electronic cigarettes. Ingesting smoke is not a normal thing for a sane human being to do.

When smoke is taken down into the lungs, there is less oxygen being inhaled. When we breathe in and fill our lungs with smoke, our brain gets less of its required fuel. This will affect the brain's efficiency, which can result in confused and irrational thoughts (panic attacks). When we are in this situation, the body can experience severe stress, and if this condition persists over a long period – as it does when a person is addicted to cigarettes – the damage and eventual breakdown of the organs affected by smoking is to some degree inevitable.

Consumption of alcohol is another abuse of the brain. I can understand the desire to shed some of the stresses that life puts upon us, but drinking alcohol is not the thing for a seemingly rational person to do. I won't go into the effect that alcohol has upon the brain, as it is widely known and experienced by a large portion of the population of the Western world each day. What I will say is that whatever the reason a person has for wanting to escape from everyday life, the consumption of alcohol is not the best way to do it. It not only has an adverse affect on the vital organs in the body but it will eventually damage the most vital organ of all, the brain.

The most laughable thing about taking this route to leave your reality is that when you come back from the drunken stupor you have induced upon yourself, you will be coming back to the exact same problems you had before you left. How's that for stupid? Maybe the next invention should be the alcohol-impregnated electronic cigarette. Then you could get out of your head quicker, with just a few short puffs!

It may seem strange to place alcohol and cigarettes in the food chapter. I did so because both smoke and alcohol are taken into the body by way of the mouth, both transport their poisons through the body via the bloodstream, and both have an effect on the body and mind, just as food does. They are also both inhibitors of appetite. The difference between eating the correct food and smoking cigarettes and drinking alcohol is that the latter two have a negative effect on the body and mind, which sooner or later is bound to end in disaster.

## Superfoods

Superfoods – foods that have excellent properties that are essential to the health and well-being of the body – are not widely known in the UK at the moment. However, they were a vital part of the natural diet for people thousands of years ago and will again be recognised as such in the future. They are at the moment readily available but mostly from specialist shops and they are expensive to buy. However, some supermarkets have recently started to sell the more popular superfoods within their whole food ranges.

You can use superfoods as an additive to normal foods or drink and also have them as a food or drink in their own right. Many superfoods have a higher content of vitamins and minerals than fresh fruit and vegetables, or fish and meat. The following is a list of superfoods and their properties:

- **Spirulina** is an ancient blue-green algae found in the tropical lakes of South Asia. It is thought to be one of the oldest food sources on Earth. It dates back some 3 billion years or more, and it is still thriving today. It contains the following vitamins and minerals:
  - o   vitamin B1
  - o   vitamin B2

- o vitamin B3
- o vitamin B6
- o vitamin B12
- o vitamin E
- o calcium
- o iron
- o magnesium
- o potassium
- o zinc

Spirulina is a good source of protein and is naturally high in dietary fibre and chlorophyll. It comes as a tablet or in powder form. Just mix the powder with water or fruit juice, and it will dissolve easily. It is an acquired taste at first if drunk on its own diluted in water, but when you get used to it, it becomes quite pleasant. Spirulina is probably the most nutritious natural food on earth.

- **Goji berries** are a good source of vitamin B1 and have a high vitamin C content. They also contain iron. In the UK they are normally sold dried, but you can soak them for a while to rehydrate them. They taste good either way. Add them to your breakfast cereal and salads, or just eat them straight from the bag.

- **Chia seeds** are the highest know vegetarian source of Omega 3 fatty acids. They are also high in the following:
  - o vitamin B2
  - o vitamin B3
  - o calcium
  - o folic acid
  - o iron
  - o magnesium

- o selenium
- o zinc

Chia seeds are high in fibre and proteins and are great to add to your breakfast cereal, sprinkle on salads, or stir into yogurts. They can also be used in baking. You can buy whole chia seeds or milled chia seeds.

- **Shelled hemp** is packed full of important properties to help with the health and well-being of the body. It is very high in protein, which is important for the growth and repair of muscles, bones, and skin. It contains Omega 3, 6, and 9 fatty acids, as well as magnesium, iron, and a high level of dietary fibre. It has a nutty taste and can be added to any meal just by sprinkling it on. It is a good all-round superfood.

- **Macca powder** is ground from the root of the macca plant and comes from South America. It contains many vitamins and minerals, including the following:
  - o vitamin B2
  - o vitamin C
  - o calcium
  - o copper
  - o iron
  - o potassium
  - o zinc

It is famed for reducing tiredness and increasing sexual libido and fertility in women, and it is also a good source of natural antioxidants. You can add macca powder to water, smoothies, breakfast cereals, or anything that you are baking.

I have highlighted just a few of the many superfoods that are available in health food shops or online. A few more to look for are wheatgrass, bee pollen, açai berry, barley grass, baobab, cacao beans, chlorella, coconut oil and camu camu. There are many more, but too many to list here. Visit your local health food shop if you would like to learn more, or you can get information online.

Isn't it strange that scientists take out all of the goodness – such as vitamins and minerals – from food by processing it and then make synthetic vitamins and minerals to put back in? What is going on here? We have only to look around to see what this world has to offer. It has everything we need in abundance, and it is the best quality that doesn't need improving. Isn't it a shame that this has all come down to money and power?

Hippocrates, the Greek philosopher (460–370 BC), said, "Let thy food be thy medicine and thy medicine be thy food." Unfortunately, today in 2016 AD, those words of wisdom have changed slightly; they now go like this: "Let thy food be made from thy chemicals and let thy chemicals be thy food." What on earth are they doing to the human race? Apart from thinking about how much profit they can make out of us, the multinational food, chemical, and pharmaceutical conglomerates do very little to promote the health and welfare of people.

## Juicing

When organic vegetables have their juice extracted, the goodness they provide to the body when that juice is consumed is incredible. There are clinics in countries outside of the Western world that have impressive records of successfully treating patients – who in many cases were terminally ill – using organic vegetable and fruit juices as a major part of their treatment. You don't have to be ill to enjoy vegetable and fruit juices, though; they taste great and are good to have at any time. Because of the high quantity of goodness in them, they are an illness preventative.

In fact, if you drink vegetable and fruit juice every day – and there are a large variety of recipes – they will help to keep your immune system in top form and prevent illness from occurring. There is no special process needed to prepare them; just wash and peel if necessary; cut to size so that the pieces can fit into the chute of the juicer; switch on; and juice away. These drinks contain all the good things that the body needs to stay healthy, and because the fruits and vegetables are raw, none of the goodness is lost.

If you are new to juicing, the first thing to do is to buy a juicer. You don't need anything elaborate or expensive to start with. It is preferable to use organic vegetables and fruit, but sometimes, depending on the season, these can be difficult to get, so non-organic is better than nothing. Always wash your fruit and vegetables, organic or not. Peel root vegetables that are not organic and also cut the top and bottom off.

When making juice, you can always mix fruit with vegetables; there are no rules or regulations as to what you put into the drink, just mix it to your own taste. The main thing is that you do it. It will make a difference to your health, and if you are consistently ill, juicing may ultimately change your life. Here is a short list of some of the fruits and vegetables you can use for juicing:

## Vegetables

- bean sprouts
- broccoli
- cabbage
- carrots
- ginger
- green beans
- potatoes

## Fruit

- apples
- blueberries
- melon
- peaches
- pears
- pineapples
- strawberries

## Salad

- beetroot
- celery
- cucumbers
- lettuce
- parsley
- radishes
- tomatoes

When you eat the kind of food your body needs and reduce the intake of foods that your body does not need, you will not only feel and look good inside and out, but your body will also become more balanced. This will help if you need to lose weight or gain weight. When you combine good eating habits with the other practises that have been mentioned so far in this book, you will be well on the way to living your life to the full.

## Key point about food

When buying food it is always better to buy organic fresh food. Try to stay away from processed food as much as possible, because your body will gain very little nourishment or health benefits from eating this kind of food. Genetically Modified food development is still in its infancy. So with regard to the unknown safety of its consumption, it is better to steer clear of this type of food for the time being.

There is a large variety of superfoods available in health food shops and supermarkets now. This kind of food is very high in vitamins and minerals and will help to supplement your diet. Vegetable and fruit juices are also beneficial to the body and will help to keep your body healthy when drunk regularly. Obesity is the fastest-growing disease of the developed world. There is no need to go on any of those so-called wonder diets; just eating and drinking correctly will help you lose weight. When you start to eat the correct food, you will also need to detoxify to rid your body's cells of chemical toxins. Drinking one or two glasses of water before you do anything else when you wake up in the morning will help you to detoxify. You must clear the toxins from your cells before they can be filled with goodness

# Chapter 6

# Longevity

So far, I have tried to show you the way to achieve a life that, if all suggestions are followed, is being lived to the full. If I could include increased longevity into that equation, everything would be just perfect. Unfortunately, I can't, and neither can anybody else. If a time comes when we are ready to live a significantly longer lifespan, I believe that we will do so naturally. It will not be a lifespan that has been forced by genetic alteration for the benefit of those who can afford it.

I know that the research being done on the telomere to stop it from being shortened each time cell regeneration takes place looks very promising, and I also know that this line of research has been patented. Call me cynical, but it looks like someone is expecting to make a lot of money from those rich enough to be able to buy the drug or application for a chance of increased longevity when it come onto the market. I doubt very much it will be available to anyone on the NHS.

We are at a place in evolution where our general or expected lifespan is what it is. Every one of us is unique; we are our own persons, and we have come to Earth with our own agenda, a plan of what we need to do during our stay here. We are given an allotted span of time in which to achieve this according to the amount we have to do. This is not fate. If we fail to achieve everything that is on the plan, an extra trip down to Earth will be on the agenda. At the moment, the average lifespan of humans is around seventy-five years, but there are people dying at all ages. This is according to how much the person needs to learn and what the plan is for that individual.

Let's take a look at why and how the human body ages, the part that the telomere plays in the aging process, and why it has a huge effect on our longevity. It is common knowledge that when the cells in our body become old, they divide and die. The information that is stored within the parent cell is transferred to the daughter cell as it is forming, and it is at this time that the parent cell separates from the daughter cell and dies. This division happens around eighty times throughout our life.

It was discovered some years ago that the information stored within our genes and passed on from the parent cell to the daughter cell is not an exact copy. A small portion of the telomere, which is at the end of a cell, is missing. Every daughter cell has a slightly shorter telomere than its parent; this reduction of the telomere is thought to be the instigator of the aging process.

When the reduction of the telomere reaches a specific size, the cells with the shortest telomere begin to change their behaviour. They slow down, and the signals that control hormone output and the immune system become weak. The cells then begin to act old. When enough of our cells begin to act old, our body ages and starts to deteriorate. This leaves us more susceptible to disease, illness, and eventually death.

In order to prevent the body from ageing, the obvious solution would be to stop the telomere from being shortened each time the cells divide. It has been discovered that the body already has a solution to this problem. We all have the ability to produce an enzyme called *telomerase*. We are born with the gene that can produce the telomerase enzyme, which can stop the telomere from being shortened, but it is switched off

Telomerase enzyme can rebuild the telomere at the time of every cell division; a daughter cell will retain all of the information of the parent cell when it divides and will behave no older than its parent after it has divided. If our cells no longer act old after division when the gene that produces the telomerase enzyme is switched on, the body should remain at the same age as it was before the cell division. Sounds too good to be true, doesn't it?

If our cells are able to stop acting old when the gene that produces the telomerase enzyme is switched on, and let's say this happens when the body is in its early thirties, then when it reaches the age of seventy-five, the body will still act as if it is in its early thirties. This means that in theory, all of the diseases that would probably have been present in a seventy-five-year-old body will be absent because the body has not actually been ageing as the years have passed by, and it is still acting as if it is in its early thirties.

Could it be true that when this gene is switched on, we will remain the same age forever and ever? I personally think not. A very large portion of the population of this world lives in poverty, blighted with disease and suffering from a very early age. If you were in the same situation as the world's poorest people, would you want to live forever? Eternal life cannot be created by turning on a switch. If we were able to acquire that much power; can you imagine the misuse that would ensue? We are already controlled by power-hungry, egotistic, greedy, violent, and selfish people. God forbid that these people could get their hand on power like this and live forever. There obviously has to be more to it than that. The people of this world are not ready for this kind of power. That's why the gene is switched off.

Short of living forever, however, I am all in favour of a developed system that would slow down or prevent the ageing process, and if taking a drug or having a medical procedure can make that happen, so be it. When this technology is available, just think of the improvements that will happen to human life on this world. Many of the diseases associated with aging would be eradicated – and of course, the anti-aging cream manufacturers would all go out of business unless they could develop some other type of product for us to slap on. I think that human life would improve greatly. In theory, we should all be fitter and healthier right up until the day.

As it happens, there is already a system available to everyone right now that will slow down the ageing process and also keep us fit and healthy. It will do even more than that. It will help you to lose or gain weight by bringing your body and your life back into balance. It will also give you the advantage of having a clear and alert mind and a more manageable stress level. All this can occur without taking a single drug or having any medical procedures whatsoever. Oh, and did I mention that it is free? It will open up your life to give you greater opportunities.

What is this secret system? It's exactly what I have been writing about throughout this book. Unfortunately, it cannot increase your longevity – nothing can – but it will give you everything that I have mentioned above. This is available to you right now, and it only requires a little effort on your part. In fact, the effort is only really needed at the beginning. Once you have initiated and embraced the few changes required to the way that you are living now, very little effort is needed. Follow the advice in this book, and you will live your life to the full.

I made these changes to my life some time ago, and the quality of my life has improved beyond all measure. Yours will too.

## More on health

Unless you are a strong-minded soul who is able to cope with this kind of adversity, being sick and miserable most of the time is not the recipe for a happy life. The trouble is, most people seem to be ill most of the time. Why is this? People all over the world are vulnerable to illness because of the circumstances of their environment and their lifestyle. Being vulnerable doesn't mean that you have to be ill; it isn't compulsory. Still, people in Western societies certainly act as if it is inevitable.

It is said that people are more likely to become sick if they live in a country where most of the people are poor and where poverty is a way of life. But things seem to have changed somewhat in recent years, because now there is just as much illness in the wealthier parts of the world. The numbers are increasing as each year goes by.

Let's think about this for a while, because it doesn't make a lot of sense ... until you begin to understand the nature of illness and its causes. We associate living in poverty with sickness and disease because of the lack of resources in many of the poorer countries. There is a lack of clean fresh water, a lack of food, a lack of housing, a lack of good sanitation, a lack of reliable weather that dictates the success of a good harvest and in some cases a lack of freedom. There are many things that people lack in poorer countries, but their general standard of health is quite good. I know that they are more susceptible to drought, famine, and wars, but that is due to the natural position of their country and also the nature of their politics. Generally, though, they don't get as many of the major terminal illnesses that people get in the Western or wealthier parts of the world.

Let's have a look at the things poorer people have in abundance, and this may give us a clue as to why they could be healthier than many people in developed countries. They have the gift of feeling that they belong in the community into which they were born, and this provides them with a greater sense of security amongst the people they live with. There is usually help on hand for those with problems, and this help comes willingly from other members of the community. A problem shared is a problem halved. There is no NHS or private medical insurance schemes for the ordinary people within poor communities, so when they are unwell, they seek the help of their local healer, shaman, or even witch doctor. This individual can affect a cure for either physical or mental problems –

Within a poor community, there is a great sense of belonging. People rarely feel alone or uncomfortable around others, and they are generally much happier with their lot. Also, knowing that within their community they are cared for gives them a greater contentment. Being happy and contented eliminates the possibility of stress creeping into their lives, and without stress, there is less chance of disease and illness occurring.

Now let's look at what the more wealthy countries have in abundance. Although people say they could always do with a bit more, money seems to be fairly abundant. If you don't earn enough money from your job, you can always get a second job, and if that is still not enough you could always borrow it fairly easily. Unfortunately when you have spent the money you have borrowed and the time has come for you to begin to pay it back, your bank balance will suffer for the length of the agreed payback terms with the lender. This can last for years, or in the case of a mortgage, many years. Being under financial pressure for long periods produces anxiety and stress within the body and mind. Prolonged stress will affect your physical and mental health and could severely shorten your lifespan.

People born in wealthy countries for the most part live amongst other people, but there is very little sense of community in their lives. This is because most people keep to themselves nowadays, and apart from the odd "good morning" or "good evening" as you pass in the street, there is very little contact with others. At one time, it was common to see next-door neighbours have a cup of tea and a chat over the garden fence, but as our society changed and women had to go out to work to make ends meet, this social pastime stopped. Women were once the hub of the family and community – in fact, they held the community together – but because of the need for more money, these social contacts are now gone. People are alienated from each other. There is a lack of communication because there is very little social contact. This can cause loneliness, and with loneliness comes anxiety, depression, and stress – which, again, affects your health and could severely shorten your lifespan.

Food is abundant in wealthy countries, but unfortunately a large portion of that food is either processed, sprayed with chemicals, or both. I know I have mentioned this in a previous chapter, but it is important enough to mention again. When we eat the wrong kind of food – and I am not blaming anyone for this, as we are given very little choice and virtually no education on the subject – we place our bodies under a great deal of stress. Many people are becoming overweight to the extent of being obese. We seem to be eating increasingly large portions of food. This is because of the addictive nature of the contents of the food we eat. In reality, although we are eating more, we are actually starving our bodies of nourishment because of the lack of vitamins and minerals in the meals we eat.

When your body is starved through the lack of nourishment from the food you are eating, the only thing to do is eat more to stop the hunger pangs from coming back. How much have you got to eat to stop this from happening? The more you eat and the bigger you become, the more stress is placed upon your joints. This may bring about arthritis within these joints later in life, leaving you unable to walk unaided or even walk at all. We can already see this happening by the number of mobility vehicles now in use.

The stress within the internal organs of your body brought about by incorrect eating will eventually cause them to break down. They have been continually starved of the fuel they need to work properly. Even though you have been "eating for England", a large part of the food you have consumed has been changed by your body from sugar into fat when it should have been fuelling your cells with vitamins and minerals. For goodness sake, please stop eating junk and eat food that contains the things your body needs. You will be healthier, you will feel satisfied, and you will stop shortening your lifespan. What more can I say?

Wealthy countries have an abundance of technology. Unfortunately, much of this is used for war or has been designed to do work that had been done by human labour. Apart from maintaining this technology to keep it in good working order and programming the computers to animate this technology into life, there is very little left for a human worker to do.

Technology is more efficient than human labour and can make components to higher specifications with fewer mistakes. This makes products cheaper to produce, thereby increasing the manufacturer's profits. Unfortunately, this eradicates any opportunity for people to display creativity or perform meaningful achievements during their working life. Large numbers of the workforce today have desk jobs for which the main task is to sit at a computer and push paper around from one department to another. No doubt this too will be automated eventually.

Many jobs nowadays do not require human intervention, and this is making those without jobs feel redundant. Taking away a person's opportunity to work will in many cases take away their sense of self-worth. With a lack of self-worth comes a feeling of disappointment and uselessness, as they are apparently unable to contribute anything towards society. There is nothing provided to replace the lost jobs, so anxiety and depression usually follows. Anxiety and depression are the symptoms of inner stress. If the unemployment is long-lasting, a breakdown of the person's health will not be far behind.

Did you notice that every case of abundance in the wealthy Western world was accompanied by lack? There is a good reason for this, as there is always a price to pay when you move away from nature. Nature can provide everything that our society needs. When we stop utilising the gifts that Mother Nature provides in favour of manufacturing our own synthetic products such as food, medicine, and chemicals, we move away from nature. The further we move away from nature, the more problems we create for ourselves.

Things will only get worse until the situation is reversed and there is a move back towards nature. There is no balance between human beings and the Earth at the moment; we are taking all we can from this world and in effect using it as we would a bank. We are borrowing all of its resources to provide the greedy with the money they desire, but we are not making any repayments. This, however, can only happen for a short time, and then we will be forced to pay it back. Many will suffer for a while, but eventually the balance will be restored, and we will once again be in harmony with our world.

In most cases, people living in the poorer countries are healthier because they live closer to nature. There is a give-and-take situation between the Earth and the people who live and work on it. The key to this partnership is giving and not always taking. It may on the surface look as though their way of life is a lot harsher than we experience here in the West, but they are in closer harmony with the Earth than we are, and they have a much better chance of living their life to the full than we do.

At the present time, we have only one home, and if we continue treating it as we are at the moment, there is a risk that it may start to rebel or break down. If this were to happen, there is nowhere else we can go. Most people believe that we are living in a world of scarcity, and that belief is so strong that the type of world we have now created for ourselves compels us to compete against each other for our fair share of everything. It is because of this belief that we have now manifested a place where there never seems to be enough to go around. We have created a situation where we are fighting each other for the things we want and even the things that we genuinely need to be able to live.

But in actual fact, this world is and has always been full of abundance, and it is situated within a universe that is also full of abundance. You have only to ask and believe that what you are seeking is what you really need. If you truly believe that what you are asking for will be delivered to you, then you will receive it. This world has been turned into a place of competition, but there is no need to compete at all. It can be turned into a world of creative thought where everybody works together. I will write more on this subject in another chapter.

## Key Points

### *Longevity*

There is much work going on trying to stop the ageing process and increase human longevity by stopping the telomere from shortening when cells divide. We already have a gene that produces an enzyme called *telomerase* that will do this, but it is switched off. Maybe it is switched off for a reason; perhaps we are not ready to live forever at this point in our existence.

Practising the teachings in this book will help to slow down the ageing process in a natural way. There are no drugs involved, so no side effects. No one can increase human longevity; it can only be increased naturally by evolution.

## *Health*

Being sick and miserable most of the time is not the recipe for a happy and contented life. It is our lifestyle that is making us sick. We eat and drink too much; we also eat and drink the wrong things. By eating too much of the wrong type of food and drinking too much of the wrong kind of liquid, we literally starve our bodies of the nourishment they need to live a normal life. If we keep eating processed foods that have had the nourishment processed out of them, we deny our bodies the goodness they need to remain healthy. We might just as well eat the cardboard packaging that the food came in.

# Chapter 7

# The three Dantians

As mentioned previously in this book. There are three areas within your body that are referred to as *dantians*. These are areas of special significance. The first, which is situated about 40 to 50 mm ($1^1/_2$ to 2 inches) below the naval and about 25 mm (1 inch) behind it, is called the *lower dantian*. The second area is located in the middle of the body just behind the breast bone and close to where the heart is seated and is called the *middle dantian*. The third area, the *upper dantian*, is positioned in the head. It is behind the forehead in the centre of your brain in an area roughly level with the temporal lobes and is believed to be associated with the pineal gland.

## The lower dantian

One of the main functions of the lower dantian is to store energy and help chi move around the body, making sure that every organ and every cell has its fair share of energy. The lower dantian is specifically significant because it not only relays chi around the body but also is the main storage area for chi within the body. It is believed to be the bioelectrical power source or battery of the body. The lower dantian is also an area of focus when meditating or practising qigong and t'ai chi, as it is where chi is generated. This is just an overview. The lower dantian has other attributes that are not relevant to this book.

As previously stated – but it won't hurt to mention it again – chi is everywhere, It is the fabric of the universe, what joins us to the universe and the universe to us. It is a huge network of bio energy that keeps everyone and everything connected. We are all a part of the universe, and the universe is a part of us.

Everything in the universe, whether it is a sentient life form or not, has energy within its structure. There are ninety-eight naturally occurring elements that make up our universe, and everything within the universe is made from combinations of these elements. We are electric beings, and the universe is also electric. The network of energy – chi – is what connects us all together.

## The middle dantian

The middle dantian is not a main storage area of energy like the lower dantian, although it does store some energy. Its function is more to do with emotional affairs, such as love, compassion, and kindness. It is instrumental in looking after the health of the organs in that area, like the heart, lungs, and thymus gland. It is an area where your chi can get very hot, and you will find that it is beneficial to bring cooling chi up from the lower dantian to the middle dantian to dissipate the fiery heat from this area.

## The upper dantian

Like the lower dantian, the upper dantian is a focus for meditational practice, as it deals with things of a spiritual nature. It is instrumental in bringing information and messages to the conscious mind. It has a connection to the subconscious mind when the higher self is communicating with it.

If you are unable to maintain the circulation of chi around your body, it will upset the balance of the body. This can be manifested as either a physical or a mental imbalance. There are many reasons for an imbalance to occur within the body; it can be triggered by any number of negative thoughts, actions, or interactions with other people. I know that I'll get a reputation for repeating myself, but I would just like to remind you that the methods of replenishing the body with chi are as follows: eating the correct foods, practising the correct exercise, breathing correctly, and maintaining a relaxed mental and physical approach to life. In this way, chi can flow smoothly around the body, and you can once again enjoy full health and well-being. If there is a problem replenishing the body with chi or the circulation of chi slows down or perhaps even stops, this is usually due to stress. Those areas suffering with stress are likely to be short of chi, and due to this lack of chi and the body's imbalance, it won't be long before they start to complain.

When there is an imbalance within the body, some of the symptoms will be tiredness, feeling unwell for no apparent reason, lethargy, headache, immune system dysfunction, and nausea. To bring the body back into balance and get the chi flowing again, start to breathe correctly (see Chapter 2), thereby bringing your body back into a more relaxed state. When you are relaxed, your stress will disappear and the chi within your body and the chi coming into the body will start to flow again. The lower dantian will relay it to where it needs to be.

When you keep the chi flowing around your body, your health will improve and you will feel good within yourself. Your dantians will continue to regulate and relay the flow of chi within you, feeding the cells of the body so that you can live a happy and healthy life. That is how the three dantians help us to live life to the full. When we play our part by doing all of the correct things, the dantians respond and play their part by keeping the energy flowing to keep us healthy and glowing.

## On another level

There's another level to the importance of the three dantians and the role they play in maintaining the health of your body. The function of the dantians and the significance that chi has not only upon the physical body but also in a spiritual sense falls outside of the parameters of this book, but I will write a short piece about the dantians and chi that you might find interesting.

Chi is energy, but not in the sense that you would think. The energy you are familiar with is energy that is used when you exert yourself. This type of energy comes from another source: oxygen. Oxygen travels through the circulatory system to the muscles to be used as fuel, which produces physical energy. Oxygen is the fuel for muscles. Under certain conditions, chi can also be used to help you move objects or perform some of the operations that you would otherwise use muscles for. Using chi in this way requires a different type of training done internally, using the mind to project the chi out and away from the body.

Chi can be projected from your body either through your hand, through the dantians, or through any other part of your body should you wish, under the direction of your mind. To control chi in this way takes many years of practice and requires the practitioner to learn soft and hard qigong, t'ai chi, and meditation. Perhaps a better use for this kind of training would be to protect your body against physical harm or to keep cool when heat becomes unbearable in the summer. When you have learned how to move chi throughout your body, it will also keep you warm in the winter. Chi can even give you the power to heal.

Therapists who use chi energy to promote the start of healing in others have to be trained to do this. Energy healing using chi has been known about and used for thousands of years. When chi is used for self-healing, it is possible with practice and by using qigong techniques to direct energy around your body, thereby promoting healing within diseased organs or areas affected by pain or infections. When you can direct chi out to your skin (skin breathing), you will strengthen your immune system, and this will protect you from illness.

Should you be unlucky enough to succumb to a flu virus or a bacterial cold infection, you can relieve yourself of them literally within minutes – not hours, days, or even weeks, but minutes. I know through my own personal training that this really does work. I haven't been ill or had to visit a doctor for at least the last twenty years, and I have never been in hospital as an ill patient ever. If everybody would adopt the training regime that I am advocating, doctors and hospitals would only be used for severe accidents, because there would be little or no illness to treat.

When you are able to use the internal movement of chi in conjunction with your breathing, it is possible to maintain an even body temperature. What I mean by this is, if you are cold, then by using your breath and chi together and directing your chi into the centre of the body you can raise the temperature of your body, thereby making you warm and comfortable. Alternatively, if you are hot, you can make yourself cooler by using your breath and chi together, projecting your internal chi out to your skin to reduce the heat within your body.

I have been doing this for some years, and I have tried to teach my family. They thought it was a joke. I taught the students in my t'ai chi classes to use this technique, but they also weren't convinced. They didn't put in the work to make it happen, so they were hot and bothered every lesson in the summer and freezing cold in the winter while I was comfortable.

If you are new to chi and the dantians, then all you really need to know at this stage is that chi is a real energy and that the dantians store chi and relay it around your body, refuelling every cell and keeping you fit and healthy. Chi is definitely playing its part in your life by helping you to live life to the full.

## Key points

There are three Dantian in our body, lower, middle and upper. They are relay stations and their job is to store life energy (chi) and distribute it around the body to keep the organ of the body healthy and in good working order.

# Chapter 8

# Abundance

The universe is thought to be mostly empty space (that's probably why they call it space), but our universe isn't empty at all. It is full of energy. It is a huge network of chi that has an effect on everyone and everything. Chi is biological electric energy that connects us to each other and to the universe. We live in an electrical universe where the fuel source for life is chi. Our thoughts are instigated by electrical impulses within the brain. Because these thoughts are electrical in nature, their frequency can be measured.

It is widely known that the frequency of a positive thought is far more powerful than the frequency of a negative thought, so everybody can, with a little practice, project the positive thoughts of whatever it is they want into the universe and receive back whatever they have asked for. Or they can ask to do whatever activity they want to do or to be whoever they want to be. Yes, this is true; the universe is full of abundance and will respond to your positive thoughts so that you can receive anything from the abundance that the universe has to offer. All you have to do is ask.

This is not a free gift, though; you will have to put in a little work to receive what you want. If you can maintain a positive frame of mind and be absolutely sure of what it is you want, then believe in your mind that you already have it and prepare yourself to receive the item physically by knowing that it is already on its way to you right now. This will cause it to arrive.

Unfortunately, there is a drawback to this system, as the universe responds to negative thoughts as well. Most people – and this seems to be quite common in human beings – find it easier to think negative thoughts than positive ones; they tend to think only about what they don't want or how awful everything is. If you project a negative thought into the universe and that is the thought you have most often in your mind, you will receive what you are thinking about, and it will be what you don't want.

A positive thought is more difficult to maintain than a negative thought, because in this day and age the human brain has been manipulated and abused by the system so much that it finds it easier to have thoughts of doom and gloom, gossip and scandal. It has become almost impossible for most people to keep a positive thought in their head for more than just a few seconds. Meditation will help; eating the right food will help; doing the right exercise will help; breathing correctly and learning to relax will help.

Look, I am throwing you a lifeline here. Live life to the full! Reap the rewards that this universe has to offer; attract the things that you want, not the things that you don't want, by using the power of positive thought. The universe is brimming over with good things and is waiting to give them to you.

You can tap into the network of chi that connects everything in the whole universe electrically, and by sending out a signal of the right vibrational frequency, you will attract the things that you want. This has been known for thousands of years but has largely been forgotten or withheld from us. It is not apparent in today's world.

## The universe and how we exist in it

The universe is full of abundance. Does anybody really know what that means? I would think that very few people have any concept of what the universe even is, let alone what it is supposed to contain. Let us try to put this in a way that can help us understand the universe a little better. (That was not intended to sound or to be condescending.)

Very few people know much about the universe, and those who do still don't know very much. This is not for want of trying. The universe is so large from our point of view that even with the strongest magnification of our biggest telescopes we cannot see the edge of it. Everything we know beyond a certain point is supposition; theorists can only speculate as to what it is like at the edge of our universe, should it not be infinite.

Many scientists only study the physical elements of the universe, and although these are important, they are missing the unseen pieces that make up the fabric of space and connect everything together. Our universe has a network of unseen substance that is electrical in nature and is joined to everything that exists. This substance is bioelectrical energy, universal energy, the substance that brings life to our universe; its electrical charge not only connects physical things together but also connects to our thoughts. Yes, this is a thinking universe.

Even if we had the technology to see and understand what it is like close to or at the edge of the universe, we would probably find that it is much the same as it is here, only older. Even so, we will never be able to see what it is like in the universe next door no matter how clever our technology becomes. It is a matter of molecular density and vibrational frequency that separates us. This universe is three-dimensional, and its molecular density and vibrational frequency is set at a certain rate and will always remain inside the set frequency of its parameters. We are living amongst other universes that share the same space as us, but because their frequency and density are set at a different rate, we are unable to see, hear, or feel them. Our universe has no compatibility with any other universe, and therefore, without our intuition, we would be oblivious to their existence.

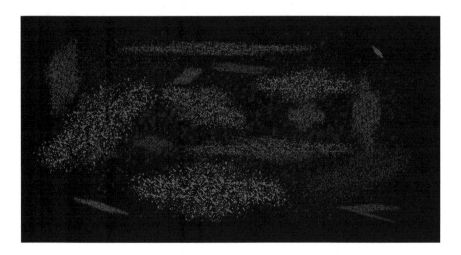

We are only able to relate to the universe we live in, and most of that is beyond our comprehension. Yet in reality there are many universes, each one set inside a huge area known as a *dimension*. The dimension establishes the parameters that the universe will operate under – for example, whether it will have three dimensions, five dimensions, or even a thousand dimensions. Each dimension will also determine how many naturally occurring elements its universe will be built from and within what range the density of its molecular structure is going to fall. Our three-dimensional universe is quite dense, with a low vibrational frequency. When you get beyond single-figure dimensions, the vibrational frequency increases, and the structure of the universe within is less dense. Our universe is built from ninety-eight naturally occurring elements; our scientists have synthesised another twenty unnatural elements

We can see the same system in operation within ourselves. Inside our flesh body resides the real person – soul, spirit, or whatever you want to call it. This entity takes up residency inside the flesh body while it is on this world. It does so because our spiritual body is unable to live on a world such as this due to the rate of its frequency, which is incompatible. Our molecular density and vibrational frequency do not match that of this planet, so without the flesh body to hold us in place, we would drift around like a ghost and pass straight through this world.

Ah, I hear you thinking, why is it then that we don't drift through our flesh body as well? That is a good point to make, and the answer for those sceptics amongst us is that the flesh body has been designed to accommodate a spiritual body such as ours, to help us achieve and overcome the challenges that a world like this has to offer. The planet Earth is a physical place in a physical universe, and it affords us the opportunity to learn physical things. Even the mental challenges are more physical here than they are where we come from originally.

Our physical body cannot leave this world, as it is of the same physiology as this world. It has been designed and made to live and operate here, and it cannot exist anywhere else. However, our spiritual body is not of the same physiology as this world or this universe and cannot live here unaided. Hence, when we are born to this world, we are provided with a physical body to use for the duration of our stay.

We are able to accommodate our flesh body because the vibrational frequency of our spiritual body has been slowed down to the minimum limit of its parameter to become compatible with the flesh body. Similarly, the flesh body has had the vibrational frequency raised to the maximum limit of its parameter. This brings the two bodies in line with each other and prevents either from drifting through or apart from the other unconsciously.

It is left to us how we use this body, as we have a certain amount of free will while we are here. Unfortunately, many people abuse their physical body, sometimes beyond repair. Our physical body has been loaned to us while we are here and is a self-contained unit that has the ability to grow, move, and maintain all of the physical functions that it has to perform automatically. It even has the ability to self-heal, but if we abuse it to the extent that we are unable to complete the tasks that we came here for, we will have to keep revisiting this world until our lessons are completed.

Many of us treat this planet as a holiday resort. A large number of people think we are all here for a good laugh, so anything goes. Unfortunately, that's not true. This is in effect a school – a place that gives us an opportunity to learn and advance. The time for a holiday is when we have studied hard and learnt everything we came here to learn, and then we can leave this place for good. It is only then that the holiday starts, and it finishes when once again it is time to move on and advance even more.

In order for us to have the best chance of completing the lessons we came here to learn, we must keep our physical body fit and healthy so it can function right to the end of its allotted lifespan. To do this, we need to live life to the full.

Okay, before we go further into this book, let's review the last couple of chapters.

## Key points

There is a huge amount of abundance in the developed countries of the world, but this comes at a price, because there is also a great deal of lack. There is some lack in poorer countries, but there is also a huge amount of the right kind of abundance: love, happiness, good health, contentment, and community.

There are large numbers of unemployed workers in developed countries, and much of this unemployment is directly related to the advancement of technology within industries. The human workforce is being replaced by machines. This can have devastating effects on the health of those people who are made redundant and have no prospects of getting any other employment.

To tap into the abundance of the universe, develop your power of positive thinking. You will also need to know exactly what it is you want and that you are worthy enough to receive it. Believe it is yours and it will arrive.

Be aware that this will also work with negative thoughts. If your prominent thoughts are negative, you will attract that negativity to you. If you keep thinking about something that you don't want to happen, then that thought will go out to the universe and you will attract that thought back to you – and the thing that you didn't want to happen will happen. Make sure that your prominent thoughts are positive, and then those positive thoughts will go out into the universe and be attracted back to you, so that whatever you wish for, you will receive. Train your mind to think positively all of the time, and your life will change.

We think we know a lot about the universe, but even our brightest minds know very little. The universe is so large that we can only observe areas that are relatively close to us. Many of our scientists only study the physical elements of the universe, and although this is important, they are missing the unseen pieces that make up the fabric of space that connects everything together within our universe.

Our universe has a network of unseen substance that is electrical in nature and is joined to everything that exists. This universal energy or chi is the substance that brings life to our universe; its electrical charge not only acknowledges our thoughts but will manifest the things we are thinking about most, whether they are material things or the values we require to improve our life.

We live for a short while inside a physical body. This body is not us; we just use it to live here for a short time. Our real body is incompatible with this world and this universe. We are from a different place where the vibrational frequency and the molecular density are different from the molecular density of this world and also this universe. If we were unable to use our physical body as a host while on this world, we would be drifting around like a ghost.

Beyond this multi-dimensional area of space is the home of our higher self and other beings that are responsible for the creation and existence of the dimensions and their respective universal contents. We, being a part of our higher self, are tethered to our higher self by a cord or beam similar to that of a satellite transmission wave that is beamed to a receiving station here on Earth. The cord or beam that attaches us to our higher self is more powerful and very much more complex than the radio waves we are used to using on Earth.

# Chapter 9

# Money

Many people think that if they had a lot of money, they would definitely be able to live their life to the full. To many, money represents the thing they want the most of in life. They place money above all other things, and it is easy to understand why, as having plenty of money eases the stress that is felt when it's absent from your life. It can take away the financial pressures that have been accumulating over the years.

It is widely thought that when financial stress is eliminated, all the problems we have will be solved, but this could not be further from the truth. Having a large amount of money can in itself be a major cause of stress. Money does not look after itself; there is constant pressure from others who would like to help you look after it. Financial institutions will be keeping an eye on how you are investing your money and offer to help you invest more ... with them, of course. The wise thing to do to alleviate this problem is to employ an accountant to look after your finances for you or pay for the services of a financial adviser to guide you. Either option requires you to make decisions and ultimately take responsibility for your own wealth.

You may not have thought of it in these terms, but like everything else of a material nature, money is only lent to us for the duration of our stay on this world. It doesn't matter how little or how much of it you have, you cannot take a single penny with you when you leave here. Money is of the same nature as this world. The molecular density and vibrational frequency of money falls within the parameters of the frequency of Earth and also this universe, and it cannot exist in any other place. Its versatility is only apparent on this planet; if it is taken anywhere else within our universe, it is worthless. It is backed up by nothing. It is not even worth the paper it is printed on, so to speak.

Yet even though people know this, they still crave it. Money is seen as the gateway to freedom, and it is the one thing that can offer countless material products to possess and endless possibilities to experience. It is easy to see why money has such power over people, and yet in a twinkling of an eye it can all be gone. Just one bad investment or a change of political power can leave you penniless.

Money is more likely to tie you down than provide an escape route to the elusive gateway of freedom. True freedom is not achieved by craving or seeking money, although money does have its place on Earth. Its liquidity flows around the planet, and its convenience allows us to trade more easily with each other. It becomes a reward when we supply goods or perform a service to others. But beyond these uses, it can become an object of greed and jealousy, and it can create a lust for power, allowing a person who worships it to dictate to and manipulate others.

Unless you came to this world intending to learn how to handle money as a part of your life lesson, money can be a hindrance rather than a blessing. If money is used unwisely, it may lead you away from the path you chose to walk when you elected to come to this world. Instead of acquiring money to help you live your life to the full, you may find that it will take you away from your goals and provide you with a life that is empty.

Money in itself is not evil; it is the evil intentions of people who are obsessed by it that give it a bad name. Do not become obsessed with money, material things, or people, because instead of attracting them to you, you will only repel them. They will always be beyond your reach.

Can you imagine a life without money? I include in this gold, silver, or in fact any precious material that could be used as currency. It's possible that you could, but the concept is frightening to most people. How would you be able to pay for food, clothing, and other essentials? How would manufacturers get paid for the products they produce or the services they provide? Would farmers have to grow their crops and rear their animals for free? Life as we know it would change radically.

Such a world is beyond the comprehension of most people. What would we put in place of money? If another commodity replaced it – let's say tree bark – we would still be in the same situation. Instead of robbing banks, people would be stripping the bark off of trees in forests. The nuts and seeds that trees produce to propagate their species would become so valuable they would be coveted all over the world by the greedy and would become the object of obsession, just as money is now. Governments would waste no time and would quickly impose a tax on nuts, seeds, and tree bark, and these would become the new money. Money cannot be replaced; it needs to be dispensed with totally, and then we could start again with a new, fairer system. I shall be taking a look at how we could survive without money in another chapter.

## The meaning of life

Almost everybody takes it for granted that they have a life and it is here on this Earth. Most people never seem to question this fact. I know that it is obvious – we do actually have a life, and we are most definitely living it here on Earth. But have you ever wondered what the reason for your life is? Is this life for real, even though it is only temporary? Or is it not temporary at all – maybe our seventy or eighty years are all we will ever have? And then what – oblivion?

Philosophers have pondered this question over the centuries, but you only have to look within yourself to realise the answer. Getting to know your self is a part of living life to the full. When you ask the question, you will always receive an answer. It may not come to you immediately and it may be a little quieter than you would expect, but as long as you are listening, you will hear it and understand it. Even amongst the clutter of the many thousands of thoughts and voices you already have in your head during your day, if you are listening, you *will* hear it.

When you receive the answer to a question you have asked, it will always be the truth. It may not be the answer you wanted to hear; in fact, you may even want to reject it totally by completely ignoring it or questioning its validity. This does not matter; if you cannot accept the truth at this moment in your life, you can allow your ego to kick in and help you justify the answer that you really want to hear. Maybe you are not ready at this stage to accept the truth. Perhaps if you were to work a little more on your ego, the truth would become apparent and more acceptable to you.

One positive thing will come out of this, and that is the fact that you were aware there was even a question that needed to be asked. A large percentage of the world's population is not even aware that there is a question; they're certainly not evolved enough to know whom to direct it to or even how to ask it.

So who should you direct your questions to? Is it God, Jesus, Mohamed, or perhaps Buddha? No, it is none of these. You may be a little surprised when I tell you that you are actually directing your questions to *yourself.*

As you go through life, the path you travel goes this way and that. It may also take you along an offshoot of the main path that goes nowhere. When you are travelling away from the path you should be on and you are evolved enough to understand this, you will become aware that something is not quite right.

There may be times when you feel you are going absolutely nowhere in life. You start to doubt what you are doing and wonder how you got yourself into the situation you are in. You become aware of thoughts that well up inside you; they become more and more regular, giving you the message that a change of direction in your life is needed. These thoughts will eventually guide you back to the path on which you should have been travelling all along.

These thoughts are guidance, and they come to you from your higher self. Throughout your life here, you will be in constant contact with your higher self, either consciously or subconsciously. While you are on this world, you are never left on your own; there will always be someone waiting to give you a helping hand when your life on Earth becomes tough enough to be unbearable. You are part of your higher self and have been sent to this world to experience things that would have otherwise been impossible for you to learn whilst living within the place that you originally come from.

By way of example, let's say that your world is a room that is 8 feet long by 8 feet wide, without any windows to look out of or doors to allow you to leave it – just four walls, a floor, and a roof. Let us also say that in order to move on in your life and evolve into a greater being, you must somehow understand what it is like outside of your room. It would be fair to say that in an 8-foot-square room with no windows or doors, there would be very little stimulus available to you, and therefore you would have little chance to experience or learn very much other than what is within the walls of your world. Hold on to that metaphor, as it is not far from the truth.

Developing a way to leave the room would be an essential activity for you. One possible way to retrieve information from outside of the room would be to send a probe outside to gather this information for you. The probe's molecular structure would have to be finer and more widely dispersed than those of the walls or ceiling, and the vibrational frequency must be higher than that of the room for it to be able to pass through unhindered. Where would you get such a probe from? *You* would be the probe. By developing the art of astral projection (out-of-body experience), you can project your spirit/soul, which is the real you, out of your physical body and then out of the room to experience and retrieve the knowledge and wisdom needed to help you evolve into a greater being.

This is exactly what your higher self does to gain more knowledge and wisdom when it needs to evolve. It sends a part of itself, a probe, to Earth to take up residence inside of a human body that has been designed for this purpose and which is more suited to the conditions on this world. The part of the higher self that is sent to the Earth is us. We are this probe.

So when you feel the need to ask a question, either directly or by way of a prayer or affirmation, you just do it. Your higher self will always be listening. It is usual that most questions are asked when you are having some form of difficulty that requires help, but you can direct your questions to your higher self at any time and the answer will come back to you via your subconscious mind. So make sure that you keep listening.

Don't be worried if you are not aware that you are allowed to ask questions. In a situation such as this, you will be guided automatically. If you are not ready to guide yourself through life at the moment, then your higher self and others will guide you through it. It doesn't mean there is anything wrong with you, it's just an indication that you are new to this realm and are not yet ready to take the helm yourself.

Everybody on this world – and in fact, everybody on every world in this universe – is, without exception, here to learn. Nobody is better than anyone else. The people who are able to guide you through life are able to do this because they have been here in this realm a little longer. Nobody is inferior; even the rich and famous and well-to-do amongst us are here to learn. They are learning how to be rich and famous or well-to-do. Many of them think they are a cut above everyone else, but they are *not.* Everyone has a turn to be rich and famous or well-to-do, so remember how they are treating the less well-off now and learn by their mistakes.

As you move on through life – not just the life you are living now but also the many other lives you have already lived – you will accumulate a great deal of experience. From those experiences, the knowledge and wisdom you have obtained will help you to steadily advance up the ladder of evolution. When you have lived enough lives and learned from a position of experience the lessons that were set for you, and when the wisdom you have gained has reached the stage whereby your vibrational frequency has risen beyond the parameters of this world and also this universe, then it will be time for you to move on and begin life again in a different universe within a different realm.

In the realm beyond this one, you will visit new worlds and a new universe that have different values and offer different challenges for you to overcome. When you put things into perspective, although you may think that you are the bee's knees while you are here on this world because you have reached the top rung of the ladder, there is always something else to learn. When you move on in your life to the next realm, you will need to start the learning process all over again, and the starting point will be the very bottom rung of the ladder. You will not take any of the values with you from this realm, as they are meaningless elsewhere. Everything you have learned in this realm will be processed and used by your higher self.

You are going to start again from the very beginning and will have no memory of any previous existence. This is essential, as there could be a great deal of confusion within your new life if you were to take with you the memories of things that you learned here on Earth. These memories will be irrelevant and have no meaning where you are going. You will be learning new lessons that could never be learned here on Earth. The universe within the new realm you are going to operates on different principles. It uses a different science than we do, which produces different technology. Even the very nature of their thinking would be way beyond even the brightest person on this world.

It sounds frightening, but you will never be on your own. Your higher self will still be with you, giving you all the help you need, especially in the beginning. The new realm you are going to is a little further up the ladder than the three-dimensional realm you live in now, but it is still low in the overall order of things, so you will still be required to occupy a physical body. The appearance of this body will be designed to suit the conditions of the world you are going to be living on within this new universe, and it will change as you go from world to world just the same as it does here. Remember, the physical body is not what matters; it is still just a vehicle. It is the real you inside that body that matters. You must still treat your new body with respect, because it will need to last you until the end of your allotted lifespan. This will apply wherever you go, no matter what body you are occupying.

The higher self doesn't live in the same time frame as you or I. Our perception of time on this world is totally different than real time, and it has to be this way. Time for us goes by slowly; seventy or eighty years is a lifetime to us, but in real time, that period is infinitely small. In fact, it is almost no time at all. Our perception of time is governed by the movement of the Earth around the sun, and we divide this period up into segments to give it structure so there is order within our life. Time for us is manmade and has no meaning elsewhere in our universe. In truth, the reality of time does not exist; it is only apparent to help us structuralise our existence and make sense of our life.

Our higher self does not exist merely in this universe. Our higher self exists outside of all the systems that are called realms/dimensions and universes. These areas are to us the whole of existence, and we have no concept that anything else could exist elsewhere – and where would *elsewhere* be, anyway? Everything that is known by anyone on Earth is within the systems of realms/dimensions and universes. To hammer the nail home even further, our knowledge of our own universe is extremely limited, let alone any knowledge of other universes that may or may not be in existence.

When put in this perspective, the arguing and war-mongering that goes on between countries of this world, the never-ending fight to be right (as nobody can bear to be wrong), and the need to grab as much money and as many material possessions by the people of those countries – not forgetting the money-grabbing, power-hungry plutocrats who run those countries and the deceiving uncaring power-craving politicians who think they rule those countries – all sound rather petty and foolish, don't you think?

As sentient beings, we should realise this and work together to improve our conditions. There is no reason we should be competing against each other. The universe is full of abundance, and there is more than enough for everyone. Instead of competing against one another, let's work together and build a paradise.

## Intuition

Almost everyone on the planet has intuitive abilities, but a large percentage of the world's population do not use this ability, and they are poorer for it. Of course, there are many reasons why intuitive ability does not play a part in most people's lives; one major reason is that intuition is not on any curriculum within the formal education system, so it is not taught to students and is not even widely known. Many people don't understand what intuition is, and if they do have any awareness it is wrongly tied up with mysticism. No wonder people say things like "I just ignore the voices in my head; otherwise, people will think I am crazy." Or "I never tell anybody about what I see in my head, in case I get carted off by the men in white coats."

In fact, intuition is one of the greatest gifts ever given to us. It shapes the life we are living while we are on this world, and it is essential for us to use this ability to stay on track whilst performing the tasks we all have during our stay here. There is no greater friend to us than our higher self; in fact, we are a part of our higher self and have been sent to this world to help further the advancement of our higher self.

Put simply, intuition is the ability to receive. We have been given the means through our intuition to receive messages from our higher self. For many people, this intuitive receiver has been either turned off or is not working properly, or perhaps it is unable to be understood or is being ignored altogether. This is a great shame, because unlike the fickle and superficial friendships we make here on Earth, there is no friendship more profound than the one we have with our higher self. Our higher self is the closest we will ever get to God while we are on this world. We have to learn to love and befriend our self before we can have a sincere friendship elsewhere. It is no wonder that there are so many unhappy and lonely people on this world today; there could be nothing worse than losing contact with our higher self.

The messages sent to us from our higher self are mainly given as guidance in case we stray too far off the path and start to drift. Those of us who are able to receive messages through our intuitive senses will realise that many are messages of encouragement to help us through the hard times we all endure when we are learning. That is why it is important to harness our ability; this world can be a very lonely place when your friends don't understand what you are going through and you have nobody else to turn to when you are struggling.

This world is not our home, so it is no wonder that many of us get lonely even when we are in the company of others. Talk to your higher self; don't be afraid to ask for help and guidance, and always expect an answer. Find some quiet time for yourself and listen. You will feel so much better when you hear and almost feel the familiar warmth, love, and kindness that is coming through from your higher self. Even if you have never tried this in your life before, you will recognise it to be a contact from your higher self, and you will understand and take comfort from the contact that you are intuitively making.

Once again, you are never alone while you are on this world. There is always someone to help and guide you. Use your intuition and learn how valuable this gift is. The Earth is a noisy place full of distractions. Quiet your mind, and your intuitive abilities will be sitting there quietly waiting for you to use them.

## Key points

Money is just a convenient way of trading with others all over the world. Instead of giving you freedom, money will make you a slave. To be obsessed with the acquisition of money, material things, or another person will slow down your development and keep you a slave until you can relinquish this obsession.

Having large amounts of money will not solve all of your problems, only your financial ones. Being financially wealthy can create as much stress as not having any money at all. This is because most wealthy people have had to compete for the money they have and will have to keep on competing to hold on to it. When money is dispensed with altogether, that is when you will regain your freedom.

Money, along with every other material thing on Earth, does not belong to us. It is only a tool which is lent to us so that our lessons can be completed. When we leave here, we can only take the knowledge and wisdom we have acquired during our stay. When it is time for us to go, if all we have learned is how to acquire money and material possessions, we will be empty of the knowledge and wisdom that we came here for. If we leave this world empty of these two requirements, we will have to return here again to relearn the same lessons.

When an economy-based society is changed to a creative society and the vices that money and possessions manifest are relinquished, that is when the evolution of humankind will develop at a faster pace than it is at present, thereby creating an opportunity for the advancement of technology and the cultivation of inner peace within everyone.

Do not take life for granted. Too many people spend their life drifting aimlessly from day to day, trapped in a hole they can't get out of because they are waiting for something to happen. Nothing will happen until they take action themselves. Do not be led around by others; stop this sheeplike behaviour. Everyone is an individual, and you should not be concerned about what those around you are doing. When you change your direction, new avenues will open up with new opportunities. Do not be influenced by what others are doing or thinking. Explore the reasons for your existence and make the effort to understand your own purpose.

We all visit the Earth many times, and indeed other planets in this universe also. There is a definite reason for visiting this and other worlds. Although we only come here for short periods at a time, these visits are not holiday breaks. This planet has been designed as a place of learning. Everything upon the Earth has been provided especially for us to use in the course of our learning. We have even been provided with a suitable body to live in while we are here, as we are unable to exist on this world without it.

Do not forget that when things in your life are not going well, you can always seek help from your higher self. You only have to ask the question and you will receive an answer, but it may not always be straight away, so just keep listening and remember that the answer you receive from your higher self will always be the truth.

When you are going through life, you should accumulate vast amounts of knowledge and wisdom to take with you when you are ready to leave. If you spend your life accumulating only wealth and possessions at the expense of knowledge and wisdom, you will leave here bankrupt. I shall repeat myself, as this also applies to the way you conduct your life: Should you decide to forsake the accumulation of knowledge and wisdom and indulge your time in drunkenness, drug addiction, or indolence, then when it is time for you to leave this world, you will do so empty.

We need to complete successfully the lessons we came here to learn in order to move on to the next phase of our life. Failure to do so will mean that we shall keep returning to the Earth or other worlds like it until such time as our lessons are completed and we are ready to move on. There is no opting out. We will keep returning until we learn.

# Chapter 10

# God

The philosophers among us have many theories about who or what God is, but amongst the speculation and uncertainty there is one thing that is absolutely certain, and that is that nobody on this world has the slightest clue of who God really is, nor will they come anywhere close to knowing the truth about God. This may sound offensive to the deeply religious, but nevertheless, it is true.

We have not evolved enough to know who God is. Even the brightest intellect whose intelligence far outshines that of the average person is still only at the lower end of the scale. If we had a ladder of evolution and it stretched one mile high, we would be somewhere around the third rung up from the bottom.

I do not mean to sound irreverent, but if this world was visited by someone who had first-hand knowledge about God, that individual's explanation of who God really is would go right over our heads. Nobody would have a clue what was being explained, as it would be outside our ability to comprehend. You could liken it to a quantum physicist explaining basic quantum physics to a goldfish.

I can imagine what you must think. What about Jesus? He came here to help us, and he is God's son. Jesus was a very gifted *man* who was sent to Earth to direct us back onto the path that we had strayed away from. He gave us clues as to where we should be heading by giving us the information in story form. He did this because we would not have been able to comprehend his words if he had told it to us straight. Jesus was not God's son; he was a highly evolved person who had been through what we are going through now, and he was sent back here to show us the way – and look at how we treated *him.*

God is so far removed from the point we are at now that he probably doesn't even know us. He obviously knows that we exist as a species that has just started the beginning of its journey through evolution, but we need to evolve an awful lot more than we are right now before he will begin to take notice of us directly. Let me show you from the viewpoint of an evolved being exactly who we are.

We are people who think nothing of lying to each other just to save ourselves. We are still at the stage where we kill and eat the flesh of other animals for our own sustenance. Most of us don't have the stomach to do the killing ourselves, so it is done for a profit by those who are more comfortable with it. Even pigeons are vegetarian (at least they used to be, until they found parts of a Big Mac lying on the pavement in the town centre). We still crave riches and material possessions, and there are many people who will knock down or walk over others to get that big promotion. Some people will knock down others and blatantly take away their wealth and possessions – and get gratification in doing so. There are yet others who are not as bold as that and will steal what they need from others by stealth.

We are wasting the resources of the Earth, which in truth have only been loaned to us. Because of our greed, we always take the line of least resistance and grab anything of value that doesn't require too much work. There is absolutely no need to use up all of the fossil fuels on the planet. We have the technical know-how to develop cleaner and more sustainable fuels for our needs, but at the moment fossil fuels are cheaper and more convenient to acquire. Plus, dare I say it, they provide huge profits for the companies that sell them. The attitude we have adopted is that it's okay, the Earth won't fall out of the sky. Well, one day it just might.

The violence and suffering that is being inflicted on others on this world has reached an all-time high. We as human beings think nothing of maiming or torturing our fellow humans for whatever reason with no remorse at all. Many perpetrators of these acts even enjoy the experience. I think it is a sad fact that we can no longer trust the leaders of this world. Many, if not all, have their own interests at heart, and many decisions that are made on behalf of the people are not necessarily made with the best interests of the people in mind.

I could go on a lot longer about the shortcomings of the human race, but I think there is enough here to make the point. I can hear God saying now, "Okay, send in the prophets and let me know when it's sorted out. If you can't trust the actions and words of the human race, just leave them alone until they realise how to behave and become evolved enough to know who they really are."

Everything that we know about religion, no matter what the religion is called, has been passed down through the ages from another human being. So knowing what you now know about humans, would you say that the religious information that we know today is likely to be pure and true? There are still some very good teachings within our religious writings, and if we were to take notice of this information and take it on board by putting these teachings into action, then the world would be a different and more pleasant place to live. We should take comfort in knowing that even in our darkest hour, the truth will always shine through.

You may ask, if it is true that God doesn't know us, then who hears our prayers? Who is listening for us in our time of need? The answer is, our God who is within. We don't have to shout on high to be heard; a quiet thought is all that is needed. When we communicate to our higher self, that is as close as we can get to God. Our higher self is a powerful being, as are we when we leave this flesh body. The more use we make of the time we have while we are here, the quicker we will learn the lessons that have been set out for us, and the sooner we will evolve and become closer to God.

Understanding who your higher self is and using the help and guidance that is on offer to you when you are in need is another component that will help you to live your life to the full.

## Time

You are now reading Chapter10 of this book, and at this point I expect that, if you have read the first nine chapters, you may be seriously thinking about living your life to the full. You may also be wondering, if you are not retired, how on earth you are going to find the time to do all this stuff and still go to work. Then there is spending time with your family, or going to the hairdressers or nail bar for your weekly pampering session. I know some of you guys like to have a swift half down the pub with your mates and would also like to be able to carry on doing the two or three other interests that you are pursuing at the moment. Well, time is a funny thing. It has become one of the most important things in the life of most people, and as is always the case, there never seems to be enough of it around. And yet time as we know it doesn't even exist.

Although time on the Earth appears to have been captured and tamed to give order to our lives, I don't think the fact that it doesn't really exist ever occurs to anyone. People still race around getting stressed out because of the lack of progress they are making. They are always trying to beat the clock because of the deadline they were given by someone who decided that they want it done *now!*

Time, as we know it, can only exist in the mind, where it becomes relative to our situation at any given moment. For time to be able to exist in reality, and for it to be measured, it needs two points of reference. The present is the first point of reference … and there are no other points of reference that can be used, as neither the future nor the past exist in what we understand as reality

It is a well-known fact that when a person is bored, or is doing a chore that he or she does not really want to do, time seems to drag. Time plays tricks on the mind by creating the illusion that it is physically slowing down, so when a chore is being undertaken or boredom is being experienced, it can seem as though it is never-ending. Yet when you are enjoying yourself, time appears to speed up, and on these occasions it gives the illusion that it is moving too quickly so that the enjoyment being experienced is over much too soon. This suggests that time is relative only at a single moment of feeling. As you live your life, be aware that you can only exist in the present. Everybody knows tomorrow has not arrived yet and yesterday is the past. You can take no action to alter your life in either of these periods, as they have no power and do not exist in the reality we know. They only exist in the mind.

Your power is in the present. Should you want to alter your life in some way, you will only be able to do so in the present. What you do in the present can reflect on what your life would be like in the future – which of course, when it arrives, will become the present. If you are the type of person who enjoys reminiscing about the past, that is fine, but if you develop an obsession about the past and want to keep it alive by reliving it over and over again, that is not healthy and is also a completely useless exercise, as it is impossible to relive. The past, when living in the reality that we are currently living, will never come around again. If it was remotely possible for you to relive the past, it would be a re-enactment performed in the present.

Your current age is measured by the condition of your mind and your body. Age has very little to do with how long you have been living on the Earth, because time, in this reality, does not exist. It is how you treat your body and your mind when you are living on the Earth that determines your age. Let me give you an example related to myself.

I am the oldest I have ever been at this moment since coming back to the Earth, but the condition of my mind and body are at least ten years younger than my actual age. This does not mean that I will live an extra ten years, as we all have an allotted time to achieve the things we have come here for. The condition of my body and mind are as they are purely because I live my life to the full. If I didn't live the way I do, my body and mind would look and act older than they do now, and I might struggle a bit as I got closer to the day I have to leave. As it is, I am confident that this won't happen; the condition of my body and mind should take me comfortably right up until the day. Remember, it is all about the body on this world. I actually do what I write about, and I write about it because it works. I want to share this with as many people as will listen; who knows, it might help change the world to a better place. It will work for everyone, including you.

I have met people who are coming up to retirement age, and they say that they are slowing down now to get ready for their retirement, and how much they are looking forward to having a rest after forty or so years of hard work. My goodness me, you don't need to slow down for retirement; you need to speed up. You are retiring from your job, not from life. When you live your life to the full, you will be much too young in both mind and body to sit back and relax while you are waiting to die. You can now get going and do all the things you have wanted to do all of your life.

Working makes it difficult to fit everything in because of the commitments you have to fulfil, but there aren't any when you retire. Your time now is your own. Come on, start to enjoy doing the things you have had to put off all these years. If you can live your life to the full too, you will remain fit, young, and healthy throughout your retirement and right up until the day you leave this world.

It is not your age that will slow you down it is the condition of your body and your mind. If you think old and act old, then you will be old. It has nothing to do with how long you have been on this Earth or the current number of your age. Every day, time within us as we know it does not exist; only the present exists. Stay young by eating correctly, keep fit by doing the correct exercise, and be healthy by living your life to the full.

## The abundant universe

When you would like to take a certain course of action that would not otherwise be readily available for you to take, or you would like a specific item that is not available to you because of its cost or its location, or if you want to change some part of your life that you are not happy with – or, for that matter, maybe all of your life – you are able to do these things by claiming your share of the abundance the universe has to offer. We are unable to physically see the abundance of our universe, so most people are either unaware that there is an abundance or they have heard of it but do not believe in its existence. When universal abundance is compared to the abundance of the visible competitive world – and I am referring here to the abundance that most people see on this world – then the abundance that is in the universe is limitless. You will be unable to take advantage of this abundance by competing for it; it will only give up its treasures through creative means.

When you compose an affirmation and affirm it to the universe, you are creatively asking the universe to provide what you request by manifesting it for you. When you affirm what you would like to have, do, or become – and you believe beyond any question of doubt that you will receive what you have asked for – you will receive it when it is ready to come to you. The universe will produce it before your very eyes, but not necessarily instantly. Manifestation is the production of something that was not physically visible before but is now present and physically real.

Universal abundance is more widely known about nowadays since the release of the film and book *The Secret*. Although they did a brilliant job of bringing knowledge about the abundant universe to the forefront of people's lives for a short while, most people have now forgotten how to affirm and manifest what they want because they couldn't get it to work when they tried it. They read the book and watched the film, and they still remember to quote the catchy name "The Law of Attraction," but it didn't seem to work for them. There was a lot of information given to people to draw them into *The Secret*, as there is with all of this type of self-help informative entertainment, but as with this and other books and films about manifesting from the universe, the information was incomplete.

It is all very well to say that the universe is full of abundance and you should send out thoughts and feelings of what you would like to have, do, or become into it, but it should not be portrayed in such a way that it makes you think you only have to wait a short while before you receive everything you asked for. There is usually a little more work to do than that. People need to know what the abundance is that the universe is actually full of. That is never mentioned. It is not full of houses, cars, jobs, sofas, money, and holidays. If it were, you would be able to see them and choose what you want, as you would from a catalogue.

Wallace D. Wattles, the author of *The Science of Getting Rich*, knew that there was an abundance of some kind in the universe, but he didn't know what it was, so he called it "formless Substance that thinks". He also knew that if you were to impress your thoughts upon this substance, you could create the things you were thinking about and manifest them into being. He died in 1911, and since then very little research into this universal substance has been done; in fact, in the present day, over a hundred years later, the scientific community is only just realising that there is something else present in the universe.

If everything present in the universe was taken away, the universe should not exist, because there would only be empty space left. But this appears not to be the case. Even when everything has been taken away from the universe and it should be empty, there is still an indication that the universe weighs something. This implies that there is still something present that nobody is aware of and which is invisible – something with no apparent physical substance that is also able to think. This invisible substance is universal energy or chi It is not a thinking substance, although it is affected by thoughts that are directed into it. It is easy to prove that chi is affected by thought and that it is everywhere. Chi is the force that is life.

Chi is what animates the universe and everything within it. It is also within the human body, and it is what the body uses as its source of healing. It is able to repair us and keep us fit and healthy. Without the presence of chi in our body, we would be dead. Chi is the abundance that is the universe. Without it, there would be nothing.

Think of chi as a vast network of energy that is electric in nature, present in the universe, and connected to everything. It also reacts to thoughts, so if you were to imprint a thought of something you would like to have onto the network of universal chi, it would react to that thought and be able, through its network which is connected to everything, to manifest a way that you can receive what you want. How is this so? I have been working with chi and teaching others how to use chi for many years. It is only the matter of proof that prevents it from being believed.

Try this simple exercise I use to teach students how to feel chi: Hold your index finger up in front of you and point it towards the sky. Do this with the fingernail facing away from you so that you are unable to see it. Now think of the area of your finger where the bottom of your fingernail goes into. As you think about this, you will notice that you can feel the area where the fingernail joins the finger even though you cannot see it. Now let your thoughts leave the fingernail and direct them straight away towards the big toe on your left foot. You should now be aware of and be able to feel your big toe, whereas before you moved your thoughts there, you were unaware that your big toe even existed, because you were thinking of your fingernail.

The feeling that you had in your finger and then the feeling that you had in your big toe was the feeling of chi. Chi follows thought. You can think of any part of your body, and chi will follow that thought and go to wherever your mind is. With practice, it is possible to project chi to any part of your body that is damaged or inflamed to promote the healing process. You can even project chi away from your body and into someone else's body to promote healing within them. By directing your thoughts, you can even project chi into the universe or take chi from the universe into your body.

If your thoughts are directed towards the universe and they are thoughts of something that you want, then the network of energy within the universe will acknowledge this thought, but you will not get what you want. This is because a single thought is not powerful enough on its own. Within that thought you need to incorporate a feeling to make your thought more powerful, and it is at this point that most people fail to manifest what they want. They fail because they don't know what a feeling is or how to produce one.

If I was to tell someone to feel something, he or she probably wouldn't know how to do that or understand exactly what I was talking about. Most feeling happens naturally; you can't make yourself feel love for a person, it is something that happens naturally or it doesn't happen. You can't make yourself feel hatred towards a person, because that happens naturally or it doesn't happen. So how can you send a feeling with your thought if you are not aware of what feelings are?

A feeling is a difficult concept to understand, because feelings are many things. A feeling can be an emotion, and emotions arise as a reaction to something that happens. For example, if you hit your hand with a hammer, the feeling that you experience is pain. Pain is a physical feeling experienced by the nervous system warning the brain that there may be some damage to your hand. You may meet someone for the first time and instantly feel love for that person, or you may instantly have a feeling of dislike for that person, or anger, or perhaps jealousy. This type of feeling is emotional and requires an action to occur before you are able to be aware of it. This is not the kind of feeling that is needed when manifesting from the universe.

When you ask the universe to provide something you want, the feeling you need to enhance the power of your thoughts and to help you manifest your desire originates in the lower dantian. Remember, this is the area that stores your ocean of chi. Be aware of this fact and think of the chi rising from the lower dantian to the middle dantian or heart centre, where it is then released with your projected thoughts into the universe.

Your thoughts should be a visualisation of what it is you want. The overall feeling you should be experiencing as chi is released into the universe along with your thoughts is one of mild elation, love, and gratitude. These feelings are produced by the expectation of receiving your request. It is the feeling of your visualised thoughts. Chi, love, and gratitude are what the universe recognises. When the release of chi, love, and gratitude coming from the heart is coupled with the visualised thought of what you want, it mingles with the network of chi in the universe. This process will greatly enhance the success of your request to be physically manifested, and it will come to you via a person or persons depending on what you have asked for.

This process only needs to be done once, but you should follow it up with daily visualised thoughts and affirmed words to the affect that you are grateful for what you already have in your life, and then you should show your gratitude for what you are about to receive by leaving no doubt that you know you are definitely going to get what you have asked for. It is important that you don't let any doubts enter your mind; really feel and live this part as if you have already received what you wanted and are happy and grateful to have it. This is obviously only happening in your head, but it is all part of the process of putting out positive thought into the universe and making sure that these thoughts are the most prominent thoughts in your mind. The network of chi works on what you are thinking about the most, whether it is a positive thought or a negative thought, so make sure you are thinking about what it is you want to be manifested for you the most. Make this your most prominent thought. Know that it is on its way to you, and make sure you are ready to receive it when it comes to you in the flesh, so to speak.

Many people fail to get what they want even though they have projected their thoughts into the universe, while also sending feelings of love, gratitude, expectation, and elation. Why should this be? There are two main reasons: it could be that they do not know about chi or understand how to project it, or that they have to struggle through life on what can only be called a subsistence level of existence. When you are living hand to mouth and life is hard and uncertain, it is easy to forget how to receive; you have become too accustomed to having nothing.

Many people are too proud or embarrassed to receive what they are being offered, even though it is what they have manifested for themselves. If you are not in the right frame of mind to receive, you will not receive what you have manifested. Once you have asked for what you want, it is not your concern to know how, where, or from whom it is going to come. It is your job to keep affirming and visualising in your own mind what it is you want and to keep doing it in the most positive way possible. Keep thinking of what it is you are waiting for, and also keep faith that the system is definitely going to bring it to you. Get yourself ready to receive and except what you have manifested, even if it does come from the most unlikely source.

When you are able to have your share of the abundance that is waiting for you, take a little time out and give some extra thought to what it is you really want. Do you know that you do not always have to choose things of a material nature? I know that it can be useful to have a little extra money or a new car or house, but there are other things available to you that can add value to your life and will help you achieve a life that is lived to the full. Peace of mind is something worth having, and it is the first subject I am going to talk about in Chapter 11.

## Key points

Our God is our higher self. Almighty God is beyond our understanding; we are too far down the ladder of evolution for God to know who we are. Our prayers are heard by our higher self.

Time is only apparent to us because it is relative to our actions. Real time does not exist in this universe.

The abundance of the universe is available to everyone but it cannot be had by competitive mean. Chi is the electricity that connect everything in the universe together it is a substance that reacts to thought and can manifest whatever we want by creative means.

# Chapter 11

# Peace of Mind

Trying to live your life to the full should not become a chore. If it does, you may be working on something too hard or incorrectly. Living your life to the full should be a relaxed affair. When all of the components I have been writing about throughout this book come together and become a natural part of your life, then fitness, health, and general well-being are raised to another level. This will increase the amount of chi in your body. It is especially important to know this because, as our physical body ages, the chi inside it decreases. So to keep your cells acting young and maintain a youthful-looking body, it is vital that you practice the components that will help you live your life to the full. When doing this, you will maintain a higher level of chi, and vitality will ooze from your very being.

Other people can notice the difference in a person who lives life to the full. They become aware of the peace that surrounds that person even when he or she is moving around or working. The peace I am referring to is of course peace of mind. If peace of mind is present within a person, then no matter what is happening to that individual externally, his or her peace of mind is always maintained. When you achieve peace of mind during your life, it is because you are living in the right way and are keeping an even temperament; that is to say, you are holding your emotions within the parameters that were set for you when you came here to live on this world. You are no longer a slave who is governed by extreme emotions; you never become too angry or too aggressive at one end of the parameter, nor do you become too docile or too weak at the other end.

By maintaining an even temperament, you can remain calm even in the most extreme and testing circumstances. Your emotions can easily spin out of control, especially in these troubled and fast-moving times. By keeping your feelings within the acceptable boundaries, you avoid any unnecessary confrontations with people who carry around with them a huge ego and uncontrollable emotions.

How can peace of mind be achieved? Amongst the components that you will be working with when you are training to live your life to the full, there are two in particular that will help you to achieve peace of mind.

**Meditation**

Meditation, the first of these components, will help you focus your mind and also control the inner workings of your body. When you are breathing correctly, you will learn to balance your energy. During meditation, the breath slows down, and this in turn slows down the heart rate and the workload of the other internal organs. The blood that is pulsing through your body begins to slow down. The metabolic activity of the body decreases, and the gradual slowing down of the physical body and mental activity creates deep relaxation. As this happens, any stress held within the body is released.

If meditation is practised on a regular basis, stress is easier to manage outside of your meditational practice, and the relaxation experienced during meditation becomes a normal part of everyday life. Correct breathing, a focused mind, relaxation, and stress release are key components of acquiring peace of mind.

## Qigong

The second component is qigong (I also include t'ai chi and yoga here). The elements that are qigong – and there are many – will help to slow down the body and mind. This is important in today's world, as there are too many people rushing around like headless chickens. They will never know true relaxation, as they are always bordering on hyperactivity. There can be no peace when you are hyperactive, so slow down. Slow is good and slow is powerful.

When undertaking the practice of qigong, the slow exercise performed in coordination with correct breathing will make the body physically strong. The gathering of chi as these exercises are practised will keep the healing energy flowing throughout the body. This will strengthen the body's immune system, and the beneficial effect that practising qigong has on the body becomes enormous.

The slow, gentle exercise – together with the slow correct breathing and the mindful focus on the qigong movements and the movement of chi around the body – will relax both the body and the mind while also releasing any stress held within. The relaxation you get from qigong is moving relaxation. To be relaxed when the body is still is very beneficial, but to be able to relax when moving is the mark of true relaxation.

Here again, as with meditation, there is a combination of breathing, focus, relaxation, and releasing of stress. When the body is strong, fit, healthy, and stress-free and the mind is focused but still, peace of mind can be achieved. Peace of mind is not some vague or mystical practice that is bandied about because it is the latest trend or the in thing to talk about. It is an essential property and a very useful quality to have in your life.

When you practice qigong, t'ai chi, or yoga regularly, you will achieve peace of mind that will never depart no matter what problems come your way – and there will always be problems, as this is the nature of learning when you are on this world. Having a mind that is at peace and that will keep your emotions within the parameters that have been set for you can help you overcome the challenges that life brings your way.

When you achieve peace of mind, you will be able to maintain complete composure and stay abreast of all situations without your emotions running away with you. This does not mean that you have become an uncaring, unfeeling, or indifferent human being; in fact, it is the exact opposite. In a situation where all around you are losing their heads, your composure can save the day. This will earn you the respect of those who were unable to control their emotions while trying to handle the situation at hand.

When you have achieved peace within your mind, take heart that you are now living your life to the full.

## Emotions

Patience is a virtue, or so the saying goes. There is a lot to be said for possessing a mind that is patient. A patient person can do things like the following:

- resist hitting the car horn two seconds after the traffic lights have turned green and the car in front has only just started to move
- endure long delays at an airport or railway station with a smile and say, "Great, there is now plenty of time for a cup of tea and something to eat."
- smile and speak calmly after hanging on the end of a telephone for twenty minutes listening to a machine repeating that there is a queue and be patient, your call is important
- explain kindly to a new student that pole-vaulting is probably not the right sport for a 25-stone person to take up

There are occasions too numerous to mention where you can have your patience tested. Possessing the quality of patience can help you achieve with ease the goal of living life to the full.

When someone exercises patience in a time-wasting or unnecessary situation and is able to maintain composure and even bring on a smile, they will easily eliminate any possibility of stress, thereby sustaining balance within themselves. However, people who do not possess this particular attribute will suffer quite considerably if patience runs thin. They may find themselves in a situation they are unable to handle, one that pushes them outside their natural operating boundaries and leads them to an extreme position where they are unable to retain an even temperament.

Losing your temper places you out of control of the current situation and can have an extreme and stressful effect on your body. The more you lose your temper, the more likely clear and responsible thinking will stop and irrational thought and actions will take over. Your heartbeat will increase and your blood pressure will rise; adrenalin is released into the body's system and the brain becomes disorientated and unable to function normally. In this situation, messages from the brain may be confused and anger may ensue, as all sensible reasoning is overridden. Placing the body under this kind of stress regularly is not conducive to a long, healthy, happy life.

To alleviate the stress caused by impatience – and indeed, impatience itself – go back to Chapter 2 and reread how to breathe correctly and how correct breathing will help you relax. Adopt a patient attitude in your life and rid yourself of the stress that impatience causes. You will then be a step nearer to living your life to the full.

### Anger

Anger is an extreme and volatile emotion that can easily rise up with very little provocation in these troubled times. The display of anger is the result of an uncontrollable reaction from a person who lacks patience and is prepared to let feelings stray outside of the parameters that provide them with an even temperament. Becoming angry increases the possibility of, and can invoke, other dangerous and unwanted emotions to back up the ego in the fight to be right.

Inability to control anger can place you in a situation that could easily be life-changing. Anger alters your thought process so that, when your mind is overwhelmed by anger and your thinking becomes uncertain and confused, the safety lock that senses how we think and act and which makes us the person we are is overridden, so the emotion that is being felt at that time becomes extreme. The mind spins out of control and is left to take whatever course of action it wants, rational or irrational. When anger takes over, you can say and do things that are quite out of character and which are usually said and done to create the most impact to the person they are directed towards.

When the bout of anger is over and reasoning returns to the mind, you may be amazed and embarrassed about what was said and done during the period when your display of anger was taking place. There are also occasions when anger can be so intense that when it takes over a person's mind, it compels him or her to commit uncontrollable acts of violence against another person. This can, if serious enough, lead to court action and prosecution for the perpetrator. In extreme cases, people may have to serve a prison sentence for their actions. Now that is life-changing.

If you are prone to bouts of anger, then the next time this emotion takes hold, recognise that the anger you are feeling is fuelled by stress, and stress is easy to deal with when it is happening to you. Take action to reverse the anger welling up inside you before the situation gets out of hand.

Try this exercise: Sit down on a chair and rest your hands in your lap, one on top of the other with the palms facing upwards. This is a passive posture that tells your mind that you are getting ready to relax, so you are less likely to want to do anything harmful. When you feel comfortable, breathe in normally through your nose until your lungs are full, and then breathe out slowly through your mouth. Do not force the breath out of your mouth, just breathe out slowly for at least seven seconds or for as long as it takes to empty your lungs. This will reduce the stress you have inside. Practice this breathing exercise five times, and you will feel that your mind and body are gradually beginning to slow down. Your heartbeat becomes slower as your body begins to relax; the circulation of blood will slow down, as will the internal organs of your body. As stress leaves your body, your thoughts will change from aggressive agitation to calmness.

This exercise can defuse any anger held within you and prevent your ego from fighting to be right. If it takes more than five breaths to calm down, then so be it; take as many breaths as you need. Conquer anger, get rid of your ego, and draw closer to living your life to the full.

### Jealousy and envy

Jealousy and envy can be quite debilitating. If you carry jealousy around with you, you will have to be on guard at all times. This emotion does not let you rest for one moment. You will always be wondering, is he or she with somebody else and are they just talking or is there something more serious going on? Jealousy is a strange emotion, because even though you may know for certain that your spouse, partner, or friend is not doing anything wrong, it is still difficult to get the feeling out of your head that there is a romantic affair or friendship going on behind your back. The jealousy of one or both partners in a relationship is one of the common reasons why relationships end.

Many people nowadays need a role model. A *role model* is someone you can emulate and who qualifies as the right person to mentor you though an activity or project and, by example, show how to achieve what the role model has already succeeded in achieving. This appears to be a necessary requirement in these times, as many people do not seem to have the ability to guide or teach themselves.

When you lack the ability to teach or guide yourself, you are vulnerable and reliant upon others to take on this responsibility. Placing too much reliance upon others can place you in a situation where you are always subservient, which in turn can lead to the development of low self-esteem. When you are heavily reliant upon the help of others, the feeling of inadequacy can mutate into envy of the knowledge, possessions, and abilities others have. It is easy to see why those who possess a talent for teaching are considered to be in a position of superiority and may give the impression of having the best of everything.

To overcome jealousy or envy, you must first recognise that you are jealous or envious. Many sufferers do not realise that they are displaying these emotions outwardly, and they are also unaware that when they do recognise these emotions, they are not the normal way that a human should be thinking or feeling. Fortunately, there is a solution to this problem. It is easy to remedy, as it is within your total control. Everybody can do it.

You must begin by initiating a correct thought pattern. Your mind must change how it thinks. You can start this process by breathing in through your nose and then breathing out slowly through your mouth. As I have said before, when you are using this breathing method, you will begin to slow down the function of your internal body. Along with the other organs, your brain will become more oxygenated and relaxed. This will promote clarity of thought within the mind, and you can develop the realisation that having jealous or envious thoughts is futile and not conducive to your development. The more relaxed you become within yourself, the more coherent your thoughts will be. Once you recognise that your mind has been immersed in these two emotions, you can begin to dissolve them with different and more positive thoughts. Jealousy and envy will evaporate like steam from a boiling kettle.

When you change from negative to positive thinking, there are various thoughts you can focus on to help you eliminate your jealous or envious tendencies. A very useful one to focus on is gratitude. Be thankful for what you have now. When you are grateful for the things you have, then even better things shall come to you in the future. Do not covet the things that others have; what they have now is not meant for you at this time. Do not be jealous or envious of the possessions, thoughts, activities, or friends of others. Everything they have now, they need to have to help them live a successful life and achieve the goals that have been set out for them.

You have your own life to live, and you may have different requirements for a successful life. Develop success by achieving your own goals, not the goals of others. Follow the path that has been set out for you. Being jealous or envious causes stress within your mind and your body. You will have to eliminate that stress before you can travel the path that will lead you to live your life to the full.

### Fear

Fear is an unpleasant feeling of anxiety caused by the anticipation of something that has not happened yet. Have you noticed that in most cases, your worst fears very rarely happen? If they do, they are never as bad as you thought they were going to be. Fear is an emotion that, if not checked, can run riot within your head, completely blowing a situation out of proportion before it actually happens. Fear can prevent you from doing things you would love to do. Fear is a negative emotion that can promote other negative thoughts to manifest inside your head. It can change a perfectly reasonable idea into the most ridiculous thing you ever heard in the exact moment you start to bring it into being.

The idea that you first thought of could still be the best idea you have ever had, but the fear of failure and the possibility of being ridiculed manifests negative thoughts in your head and prevents you from even starting the project, let alone bringing it to completion. There are many people who would love to travel, but their fear of flying – or of the possibility that the ship might sink, or that they might be accosted by foreign bandits or terrorists – prevents them from doing so. You could be having the time of your life if only you were able to rid yourself of fear.

In truth, there is only one thing you need to fear, and that is fear itself. There is no greater enemy than fear, so eliminate it from your life and you will be able to do anything or be anyone you want to be. Every one of your ideas will be the greatest you have ever had – and if one of them doesn't work, who cares? Push it aside and move on to the next. Travel the world and experience the different cultures that the world has to offer. You may never get another chance, and you will have no chance at all if you let fear dictate and limit what you can do in your life.

How can you eliminate fear from your life? Well, dare I say that fear is another form of stress? The same is true for all the negative emotions people seem to carry with them in these times. The way to release this stress from your mind and your body is to change the way you are thinking. You must bring your mind back to the point where you have clarity of thought and clear reasoning; until this happens, nothing can change. Clarity of thought and clear reasoning will help you see the folly that is your life while it is under the influence of fear.

This condition is easy to change, I have already mentioned this same solution to remedy other conditions several times in this book, and I will continue to mention it now and also in the future, because until you can remember to practice it without thinking, you will keep suffering from stress no matter what the condition is called. Relaxation is the solution for stress, and the catalyst for relaxation is breathing.

Breathe in through your nose normally and then breathe out slowly through your mouth for about seven seconds, or for as long as is comfortable for you. Repeat this exercise until you feel your body becoming relaxed and your mind releases the fear within. Once oxygenated, your brain will be fully equipped to regain clarity of thought and reasoning, which in turn will enable you to see how foolish you were to let fear control your life. Fear is the only thing you need to fear. Eradicate all negative emotions from your mind, and you will be on the way to living your life to the full.

## Love

Love is a positive emotion, and although it is generally thought to come from the heart, it doesn't. Love comes from the brain, and it is the brain that generates a chemical signal that make you understand that it is love you are feeling. When you feel love towards another person, animal, or treasured possession, the feeling that is experienced is a chemical reaction from the head and not from the heart, as you would expect. Although love is the most powerful of all the emotions, it can frequently be transient or fleeting – hence the high rate of divorce throughout the Western world. It is now becoming prevalent in all parts of the world.

When a person directs hatred towards you, you may feel extremely uncomfortable, but this can easily be turned around with just a few words and a few sincerely expressed gestures that indicate that your intentions of kindness and love are genuine. By using gentle tones of voice together with gentle body language, and by directing these sensory signals towards the person who is generating the hate, you should be able to create a change. This action is enough to encourage the person with the problem to consider how he or she feels towards you by persuading him or her to have a change in thinking. When hatred is overturned, the signals transmitted from the head of the person with the problem should begin to change as a new overriding signal from the brain is transmitted to that person.

Love is always stronger than hatred or anger. The latter are negative emotions, but love is a positive emotion. Although all emotions are controlled by the brain, love can be more persuasive because people generally prefer to be loved rather than disliked. Unconditional love has the same power as romantic love but is less transient. Unconditional love can last a lifetime; no restricting situations arise because this love is unconditional. With unconditional love, you are prepared to look beyond the surface flaws and shortcomings and love the person for who he or she is.

## Gratitude

Gratitude is a positive emotion and a very powerful one. Being thankful for what you already have will open the way for you to receive other things that you would like to have. A person who shows gratitude to others for what he or she has received as a gift or a service will never be short of friends. People like it when a person is grateful; they feel appreciated. If you help somebody who is in trouble and that person is grateful for the help, you will receive a heightened experience within you as your vibrational frequency is raised. It makes you feel good when you help someone; it is a little reward that you receive for being kind.

If you do not display signs of gratitude and can't be bothered to give help to others in need, you will not receive any reward, and your life will be the poorer for it. It will also be more difficult for you to receive help when you are in need if you are not showing genuine gratitude outwardly.

Some people shun help from others; this could be interpreted in many ways. Perhaps they are too proud to accept help because they are unable to show gratitude and find it difficult to give help because they are unable to accept gratitude from others. Too much pride is a negative condition that should be worked on. Keep pride within the parameters set for you. Saying thank you sincerely is a positive action and will bring rewards. Saying thank you as an empty gesture will bring you nothing.

I say thank you all the time, and I sincerely mean it every time I say it. Try it yourself. Even if you think what you are saying it for is insignificant, say it anyway. You'll feel much better for it.

Emotions are the tools that guide your life. Not everybody comes with the same emotions enabled; it all depends on the lessons that have to be learned while on this world. If you are able to keep the emotions you were given under control and maintain them within the parameters that have been set for you, your lessons will be learned a little more easily. When you become emotionally unbalanced, some work may be needed to bring your emotions back into balance. It is not wise to live your life on the edge; you have nothing to gain from being too extreme. Stay within your parameters, and it will be a little easier to achieve a life that is lived to the full.

## Key points

Practising Meditation and qigong are a good way to achieve Peace of mind. When you have peace within your mind you have gained the ability to keep your emotions within the parameters that have been set for you during this life upon the Earth. Keeping an even temperament is a step nearer achieving a life lived to the full. When our emotions whether positive or negative are left to run wild. They will move outside of the parameters that have been set for us. This extreme position is fuelled by stress and can be alleviated by the simple breathing exercises explained throughout this book

# Chapter 12

# Lifestyle

Within us, we possess the power to direct our own life. This is called free will. The extent of free will that most of us have is limited; that is, it is not total free will. We have been given the power to choose our own lifestyle and to live it on a day-to-day basis, but there are limitations as to how far we can exercise these choices. We cannot interfere with the lessons that we have come here to learn, as they are the main reason for being on the Earth.

For example, let's say that you have chosen to live the lifestyle of a wealthy person, but the actual reason you have come to the Earth is to experience the lifestyle of a poor and underprivileged person who is living in humble circumstances. Straight away, you can see that there is a contradiction between these two lifestyles. You cannot be financially wealthy and financially poor at the same time. If you choose the lifestyle of financial wealth, you will not learn the correct lesson while you are living this particular life. You would be travelling on the wrong path. In a case such as this, the chosen lifestyle could not be permitted for obvious reasons.

It is true that many people would say they have not chosen the lifestyle they are living at the present moment. I am sorry to say that they are wrong. The lifestyle you are living right now is based on the thoughts you have been thinking up until this moment. When you are able change your thoughts to a more focused and positive line of thinking and maintain what you are thinking about over a period of time, you will start to live the lifestyle that you are thinking about the most, providing it is not in conflict with your life lessons.

I can imagine that after reading that last paragraph, many of you are saying, "That is a load of rubbish. It certainly doesn't work for me. I think about changing my lifestyle all the time, as I am not happy with the lifestyle I have now, and it just does not work." Well, let me ask you a question: Have you really been committing your thoughts totally to changing your lifestyle? Have you really been committed to, and focusing hard, on the lifestyle you want to live? Are you aware that you should be grateful for what you have at the moment, or are you always moaning about your present circumstances? Are you also unhappy with the things you have now and moaning about what you would like to have but haven't got? Thoughts like these will not help you to get what you want; they will only give you more of what you already have. Thinking unfocused negative thoughts will only drive what you would truly like to have further away from you.

For many people, having focused thoughts seems to be impossible. They allow their mind to be bombarded with random thoughts throughout the whole of their life, so there are never any spare moments left to focus on what they truly want. Within their random thoughts, you will find thoughts of what they would like to have in their life, but these are not focused thoughts. They are just random thoughts like all of the others, and that is the difference.

All through this book, I have been writing about what you should bring into your life in order to live it to the full. Within these pages, there is help and guidance about how you can, amongst other things, learn how to focus your thoughts. Those of you who do not have the lifestyle that you want do not have it because you do not have focused thoughts. Many people – but probably not those who are reading this book or books like this – do not have focused thoughts because they are new to this realm (universe) and this world in particular. This doesn't mean they are inferior to everyone else; it just means that at this stage of their existence, there is a little more guidance provided, which will help them to become accustomed to the ways of this world and this realm. The free will that newcomers have been allowed is a little more restricted, and many of the decisions they have to make will normally be made for them until they can find their feet, so to speak.

There is no excuse for the rest of you. The way to focus your thoughts is in this book; learn it and you could be living the lifestyle you want to live. This will make the life lessons you are learning while you are here a little more pleasant, and it will bring you another step closer to living your life to the full.

People who are at the early stages of living their life to the full may well find that this involves enormous changes to their lifestyle – so much so that achieving their goals in this life may seem not only daunting but almost impossible. Nothing is impossible for the person who is focused and decides that this is truly what he or she wants. Remember, you cannot walk a thousand miles in one day. You have to do it a few miles at a time. Developing a focused mind and changing the way you think is a very good start to getting the lifestyle that you would like to have.

## Newcomers

Have you noticed during your present visit to this world that the population has been escalating out of control? Many people say that it is because we haven't had a world war for a while; others say that it is because the world's population is living longer. These things are true, but they're not the whole reason for this population explosion. The number of people who die from illness every year is far greater than the numbers of those who died in both world wars. In fact, more people die from malaria, cancer, and heart disease worldwide every year than in most of the wars that have already been fought when the numbers are joined together – yet the population keeps on growing. It is not the dying that should be of concern to us; the number of people being born worldwide should concern us more.

This world is soon to reach a period where there are going to be great changes. A new era is approaching, and the way that this world is operating at the moment will soon end. Opportunities for new people who want to come here and learn from the curriculum that is being used on this world at the moment will soon be gone. Here in the UK, we have schools that, for whatever reason, can be closed down by the educational authorities and then opened again with a different status. You could liken this world to a school, and this era – or school term – is almost over. When the school reopens, there are going to be changes to its status.

By way of an example, let us say that there is a school which is at the moment catering to young children between the ages of six and eleven years and which has been earmarked to be closed down by the authorities. After certain changes that need to be made to the school are finished, it will be reopened as a technical college.

The curriculum the younger students were being taught before the change of status will no longer be used. The new students coming to the technical college to learn are between 16 and 20 years old and will be taught from a curriculum made up of different subjects and that are more suited to this age group.

This world is very similar to the example given above. It has been the subject of many changes in its previous existence, and it is fast approaching a time when it is going to change again. The curriculum that is being taught now will no longer be in use. There will be a new curriculum that will suit the new occupants, who will be coming to this world after the worldwide changes have been completed.

Due to these forthcoming events, there has been in recent years a large influx of new people coming onto the Earth. They are coming here to learn from the curriculum that is being used here in the present day, hence the population explosion. By *new* people I don't mean people who are returning to the earth again to learn something new but people who are completely new to this realm – people who are new to the universe in which our world is situated and who have no knowledge of our social ways or technological advancements.

Normally, those who have come to this realm for the first time would be gently filtered in and would start their learning period on this world by living with indigenous tribes throughout what is called the Third World. After many lifetimes have been lived and the newcomers have learned how to live amongst human people, they would earn the right to make their own decisions by free will and make their own contribution to society. They would then begin to be reborn into the more technically advanced societies of this world. After many lifetimes of learning all the lessons presented to them and every advancement this world has to offer, they will be ready to leave this realm and start a new life in a new realm in a completely different universe, always advancing and striving to climb higher up the ladder of evolution.

This is the normal process of learning that has been used over hundreds of thousands of years to maintain an even balance upon this world. By this, I mean that there are always new people coming onto this world, usually in small groups and in numbers proportionate to the general population. Unfortunately, things are due to change soon, and when the present era comes to an end, the changes made here will alter the world beyond all recognition. Consequently, there is a big rush to get as many new people onto the Earth as possible before these changes are implemented. This will be their last chance to experience the life of humanity and learn how to overcome the problems humans are designed to encounter while living on this world. So now they are being pushed quickly through the system to learn from the curriculum that is in use now. This unfortunately has led to the situation that we now find ourselves in on this world today.

The world has become overpopulated, and the newcomers can no longer be situated within indigenous tribes as they were previously because these tribes are mostly extinct or have been exposed to, or already absorbed within, the Western culture. Due to the technical advancements upon this world, the so-called Third World countries are quickly obtaining the same technology and opportunities that countries in the Western world already have. This means that the newcomers who are newly born to this world, and who have now been dispersed amongst the people of the Third World, will also have access to this technology. Unfortunately, they are not yet ready to handle this advancement.

One could liken this situation to giving a 3-year-old child the keys to drive a Ferrari racing car. This is a huge jump up through the system for the child and is happening before he or she is ready to fully understand it. You cannot attend a nursery school as a 3-year-old and on your first day there be elevated to the top form of a grammar school. The lessons would be way beyond the 3-year-old child's comprehension. This is what's happening to the newcomers here upon the Earth.

We have now reached a situation on this world where these new people are being born into the technically advanced Western countries of our world. This has been the case for some time now. Unfortunately, they have not learned how to behave within these Western-based societies because they have no former training.

They have been allowed to handle technology that they are not ready for and are using it for their own ends and not what it was originally designed for. Because they were unable to go through the learning process that the present-day people of the Western societies have been through, they are now causing havoc throughout our world. Just look around you. What kind of place are we living in now?

Through their guile and duplicity, these new people are taking top professional positions throughout the world. These positions are not just in the criminal world but also within political and business arenas all over the globe. I have already mentioned much earlier in this book what is happening within the pharmaceutical industry, food industry, chemical industry, and medical care industry, and also many other industries throughout the world whose businesses are being run with the sole intention of making as much money as they can. Don't get me wrong here, there is nothing wrong with making an honest profit or earning a good living, but the present-day multinationals that are the backbone of their nation and the champions of national pride have been infiltrated and are now being operated by people of a low moral standard who have less than their fair share of scruples.

What kind of people would put addictive chemicals within the ingredients of manufactured foods in order to get people to keep coming back to buy more? These people are using the ordinary person in the street as a good source of income. Ordinary unsuspecting persons have become reliant upon these conglomerates for their food but also for their health and well-being.

It is easy to see that the system of learning that is being used on this world must be flawed, because it is leaving itself wide open to the infiltration of people who are not ready to learn from what it is now on offer. The people I am referring to are those who have come to this world from the lower realms (a universe from another dimension) and, on arrival, are being born directly into families who are members of this world's technically advanced societies. These events are unprecedented and are now happening throughout the world every single day. New people are coming to this world in vast numbers, and it would seem to be without the need to go through a learning process that would teach them about this world's societies and how to behave within them. They should be learning these beginners' lessons before they are allowed to work their way up through the ranks.

Newcomers are being allowed to gain top positions within industry and politics throughout the world without gaining a basic knowledge of social living or acquiring the foundations of decency and integrity. They are not even trying to hide this fact, nor do they care about the way that they operate or present themselves professionally. It is blatantly obvious what is going on, and it is happening today for all to see. What they are doing is affecting our world with their antisocial behaviour and craving for money and possessions. This is directly affecting and altering the way that others – that is, people who have gone through the complete system with many hundreds of visit here – are able to live their lives.

These individuals are making the ordinary people of the world dependant on their products, and the way they operate within our society allows them to force upon us policies that will benefit themselves in order to maintain whatever power they have. Their priority is to make as much money as they can, from whoever they can, whether it is beneficial to our society or not. Their behaviour will be the catalyst for the changes that are going to happen on this world.

## Change

A question asked many times is, "In what way is our world going to change and how will it affect us?" Many people presently living on the Earth are now living their last lives here and are shortly due to move on to the next phase of their existence. There are those who have been coming to the Earth, and worlds like it, for many lifetimes. They now find themselves at a point where they have finally accumulated and absorbed all of the knowledge they need and have acquired enough understanding of the opportunities that have been available to them over millennia from this world and also from the universe itself. It is almost time for them to move on. They will be the new people on the worlds in the next universe, beyond this system, where they can continue to learn lessons that were not available to them in this, their present universe. Remember, we are the probe of our higher self, and it is our task to continually accumulate the knowledge and wisdom that is on offer wherever we go.

It is my understanding that those people who are left on the Earth will carry on living and learning the lessons that have been set for them for many generations to come, but as this era nears its end and the grip that humanity has on this world starts to loosen, the human race will start to decline quickly, until human life on the Earth is no longer sustainable. Now would be a good time to start living your life to the full. This world will, over many millions of years, go through the changes that are necessary to prepare it for the next occupants. The human body will no longer be used on the Earth; it will be replaced with a body that is more suitable to whatever condition the Earth presents itself with.

The reign of modern man and woman (Homo sapiens), started around two hundred thousand years ago upon the African continent, gradually spread to every part of planet Earth. About twelve thousand years ago, humans began to develop the modern farming techniques of which the main principles are still in use today. As humans gained control over the land, they started to domesticate animals for food and to do the heavy work on the farms. The tribal way of life ended, and people were able to settle down into more stable communities. Communities started to grow quickly because of the plentiful food supply and the added sense of security within the community. These settlements continued to grow right up to the beginning of the industrial age about two hundred and fifty years ago. It was then that the size of settlements all over the world grew to a scale larger than ever before as the world's population started to escalate.

The technical advancements from these times changed everything. Human beings began to plunder the Earth of its resources in order to satisfy the insatiable needs of the people, and they have been plundering the resources provided by the Earth ever since. The resources I am referring to are those allocated to everyone in order to help each of us learn the lessons set out for our many visits here. These resources have now begun to run down. This does not mean that the Earth is running out of resources; it just means that the resources allocated to humans have almost reached their limit.

When the time comes and the human race has had its day, the Earth will shake and rattle, turning itself inside out. The surface will sink, and new resources from deep within the Earth will rise to become the new surface. This process will take place over a few million years, and when the Earth is ready to accept its new occupants, it will settle down and a new race of people will come to live upon the Earth. They'll be much the same as us, but the design of the body that they occupy during their stay here will be different from that of a human body. The design will be made to suit the conditions upon the new Earth. The Earth's land mass will be unrecognisable to us if we return here, and the human body will be unable to breathe the air of the new Earth. The proportion of gasses that make up the atmosphere will be arranged differently than they are today.

Although the reign of the human being may be at an end, that does not mean that we as spiritual beings will also die; far from it. The human body was designed as a carrier for us to stay in when we needed to visit this world. It was designed to cope with the conditions that the Earth presents at this time. It is a vehicle that is only loaned to us – that is, the real spiritual us – to travel around in and to help us complete the lessons that have been set for us during our visits here. Anything and everything that happens to the human body while we are occupying it during our stay here is for our benefit, whether it be a pleasant sensation or otherwise.

In order to break the repetitive cycle of birth and death, it would be wise to begin today living your life to the full, so that you can move further along the path of evolution. You will reach a stage eventually when you will be able to dispense with the need to be contained inside a physical body in order to learn, and you will make further progress wherever you travel as you truly are.

## Positive thinking is the way ahead

Have you noticed how almost everyone complains about what is happening in the world today? What a terrible world we live in. They also complain about the things that are happening to them within their own life and how much happier they would be if only they had more of this or more of that, a better job and bigger house with happier neighbours.

Many people complain that they have more than their fair share of problems. They think that calling problems a "challenge" will somehow alter the impact of the problem. Well, it doesn't. The problem remains with them until it is sorted. They do not understand that whatever they are complaining about has been invited into their life by themselves.

You may be reading this for the first time in this book, but it is a proven fact that we live in a thinking universe. That is, the universe we live in responds to our thoughts. Whatever we think about the most will be manifested into our life. It has become apparent to me of late that many people on this world – in fact, a great many people on this world – have adopted a negative pattern of thinking, and they are able to maintain this negative train of thought throughout their lives. This is incredible and is an achievement worthy of note because more energy is expended when a negative thought is produced than when a positive thought is produced. It is no wonder that half the population is tired for much of the time and also laboured in thinking and activities.

Do yourself a favour and change the way you think so you can learn the lessons you have come here to learn without any adversity. Negative thinking will always bring you what you don't want – that is, if what you don't want is what you are thinking about the most. There is always an association with having to cope with endless problems if you have a constantly negative thought pattern.

Hope is on the horizon. Practice the lessons in this book, and when you are able to adopt a positive thinking pattern into your life, you will enjoy and benefit from the learning process much more. If everyone living on the Earth now was to adopt a positive thinking pattern, then this planet would be a paradise and not just a school. There would be no need for the planned changes to go ahead.

## Key points

Although we have free will while we are on the Earth it is not total, there is a limit to the choices of lifestyle we are able to choose. If our choice of lifestyle is in conflict with the reason we are here then a different lifestyle will need to be chosen.

People ask what will happen to them when the world changes. The short answer is nothing; our real body will carry on living and learning somewhere else. Remember we are the probe sent out by our higher self to learn and experience the thing that the higher self is unable to.

The way that many people use their mind seems to dictate the lifestyle they lead. Negative thinking will always get you what you don't want. The more you think about what you don't want the more you will get what you don't want. Do yourself a favour think more about what you do want and your life will change accordingly

# Chapter 13

# Birth and Death Cycle

At this point in our existence, we are in what seems to be an endless cycle of birth and death. I know that many people believe the life they are living now is their only life, and that is fair enough because most of us have no recollection of any previous lives or prior knowledge of the lives we may live in the future. However, the truth of the matter is that we do have to live many lives, but not just on this world; we also visit many other planets within our universe. This is what we do. This is our reason for existing apart from our higher self. We are the probe or the instrument that is sent out to places which are inaccessible to our higher self. We go to many different worlds to collect the secrets held within this universe in the form of knowledge and experiences that our higher self has no other way of acquiring.

The number of lifetimes we have to live in this universe depends on us. If we knuckle down to the tasks at hand and complete the things that have to be learned without any glitches, we will live fewer lifetimes in this universe. There will be no need to keep returning to Earth to retake any unlearned lessons. If we are able to remain on our chosen path throughout our life here, we will be ready to move on to the next universe much more quickly. If things do not work out as well as we would like them to, we'll need to continue the cycle of birth and death here until our job is completed. Only then will we be able to move on to the next stage of our existence.

What situations are we most likely to encounter that will prevent us from moving on in life? A breakdown of the connection between you and your higher self is one problem. If you are unable to be guided through life by your higher self or by others who are always on hand to help you, then you are likely to drift off your chosen path, especially if your life starts to become difficult. One of the problems humans have today while on this world is lethargy, and it is difficult for many people to overcome this condition without guidance. It is in our nature when under pressure to take the least line of resistance, but this will undoubtedly lead us away from the path we should be travelling on. Taking the easy way out is rarely the right option.

A breakdown of communication between you and your higher self can occur when the intuitive connection is broken or ignored. If you are not listening to the messages of guidance sent to you by your higher self, how are you going to know what to do next? It doesn't matter whether you are rich or poor, or whether you think you are totally in control of your life – if you ignore your intuition or the connection breaks down between you and your higher self, you will stray from your path. This may lead you to become confused and disorientated. If you are not going in the right direction, your life here will be wasted. You will be unable to complete any of the lessons you came here to learn.

Guidance is the most important thing to understand. Even the world's most powerful leaders and their advisers need the guidance of their higher self; ignore this at your peril. If you let your ego get in the way by thinking that you do not need to be told what to do – if you try to go it alone – you will find that you have made the wrong decision and your visit here this time around will be wasted. No one can drop out of the class. You have to learn and experience the lessons for which your higher self sent you here. If you fail to do so, you will have to come back again and again and again to learn the same lessons until your task here is completed.

Another way you can become distracted from the guidance of your higher self and other guides is if you do not have a strong foundation. Without a strong foundation, you can easily come under the influence of those who do have a strong foundation and a stronger mind than yourself. Such a person as this may have a strong mind, but usually they are also ruthless and have low moral character. They take delight in influencing those they consider to be weak by guiding them away from their task and manipulating them. People who are most likely to fall prey to this kind of influence are those who are new, or fairly new, to this universe and who have not yet lived enough lives to be able to deal with this or to build a strong foundation.

All is not lost, though. There is always payback for people who behave in this way. Nobody can escape from their karma, no matter how strong they think they are. If you mislead or harm other people or any living thing for your own gain, you will have to pay for this wrongdoing. Usually this payback comes from suffering some injustice yourself and also by having extra lives added on so you can iron out any nasty traits you may still have. You can see from this small example that the number of lives you have to live before you can break the cycle of birth and death in order to leave this universe is entirely up to you.

For those of you who have just started to live your life to the full and those who are already living that way, take heart. By now your inner foundation should have strengthened, and your vibrational frequency will have started to increase. You should be well on the way to breaking the cycle of birth and death in this realm and also coming to the end of your human existence.

## The basic meaning of karma

The word *karma* is widely misunderstood. It is not generally known in the Western world, but many of those who have heard it believe it to mean 'fate'. This is the wrong interpretation of a Sanskrit word from the ancient Indian language; it actually means 'action'. Karma is a law inflicted upon one's morals. There is also a strong belief that karma is a punishment or an infliction of suffering placed upon a person for wrongdoings, and to a certain extent it is. But there is much more to it than that.

Karma is, as explained in Buddhist text, the law of cause and effect. If you cause harm by physical or mental means to another person, animal, or any living thing, the consequence of that action will have an effect upon the life of the perpetrator also. This effect is tantamount to, or maybe even more severe than, the suffering inflicted upon the victim.

As with yin and yang, everything must have its equals and opposites, and karma is no different. For every wrong that is committed, the opportunity to help somebody else is also present. On the occasion that an opportunity presents itself to give help to someone in need of assistance, the mere fact that a good deed has occurred triggers the law of cause and effect.

Karma not only takes the appropriate action when someone has inflicted harm, it also takes action upon someone who has performed a good deed. This reward is not repaid by the person who has just received help, and it is not a like-for-like repayment. It comes to helpers at an appropriate time, usually when they are in need of some help themselves.

No one can escape from his or her karma, as it is an automatic process. There is no one looking at your every move waiting to judge your indiscretions, nor is there anyone getting ready to punish you for your misdeeds. It is also believed, and wrongly so, that whatever harm you may have caused to others in this life can only be paid for in the next life. This is not so; if the condition in this life changes and an opportunity presents itself and gives you a chance to make amends for the consequence of the action against the victim, then payback for the harm that has occurred can be rectified in this life. The payback in question can happen on the same day of the incident or at some time in the future when the conditions are favourable for the wrong deed to be paid for by karmic action.

As you can see, there is nothing mysterious about karma; it is just the law of cause and effect and can be explained in a couple of pages. Everybody should be aware of the effect that karmic action has upon their lives. If you can read and understand these few lines about karma, you should realise that it does not pay to harm any living being, as the reprisal can be more severe than the actual harm imposed upon the victim. If you are able to help someone in need by doing them a good deed, you will find that it is much more gratifying. It not only lifts your spirits by increasing your vibrational frequency but also, when you are in a situation where you need a helping hand yourself and the condition is appropriate, help will be at hand.

Being aware of your karma can help you take the appropriate action throughout your stay on Earth. When you take the right course of action, you can be sure that you are on the way to living your last few lives here. Understanding the karmic law brings you another step closer to living your life to the full.

## Religion

Religion plays a large part in many lives, but even though the teaching of the major religions is forgiveness, in today's world many people find it difficult to forgive. The stress of living on this world and the strong feeling of aggression amongst people seems to have hardened the heart and the attitude of many, and they can no longer find forgiveness for others within their heart. This may be the reason that, in recent years, religion has been declining in popularity.

There seems to be an ever-growing number of people who believe that God does not exist and when you die, that is it, you are dead. This is understandable, because from their point of view nobody has ever come back from being dead, even though there are many rumours and many written accounts of this happening in the past. These events never seem to happen now in today's world – and there has never been, to my knowledge, a physically witnessed case of a person coming back to life a year or two after he or she has died to show that there is life after death.

Why? What has changed over the last couple of thousand years that prevents those who have died from coming back? If it was commonplace thousands of years ago, then why isn't it now? If someone could come back in person to the Earth and prove that he or she is still alive, surely that would help a lot of people overcome their fear of death. If everyone knew they were not going to die permanently, surely that would be a great comfort and would also help them complete their tasks here more easily and without fear. In the great scheme of things, I'm sure that it wouldn't cause too much trouble if God were to send back a few people every once in a while to give proof that nobody is totally dead when they die; they're actually still very much alive and enjoying an existence somewhere else. That would be helpful, wouldn't it?

The truth of the matter is that it was not commonplace for people to come back from the dead thousands of years ago, or ever. Such reports are a myth. Once the Earth body dies, it is permanently dead, and after six hours or so it starts to decay. It can never be recovered from this state and be reused. Fortunately, the Earth body you occupy while you are staying on this world is not *you*. You are the spark of life inside. The spirit that occupied the human body for a short while in order to learn what this world has to offer will leave it when it dies.

You – the real you – will never die. Every time you come back to the Earth to start a new period of learning, you will have a different body. You will be born into a body that is suitable for the life you are going to lead during this visit. While you are here, you will remember nothing of your previous life. The body in which you stayed the last time you were here no longer exists.

Every human body, without exception, has a shelf life, and once it has reached the end of that allotted time and is of no further use, it dies. At this point, you are set free. The laws and restrictions that were enforced upon you during your stay upon the Earth no longer apply. Whether you were a religious person or an atheist, a world leader or a road sweeper, once you have left this world you are free from whoever you were.

Religion came about when human beings lived in tribes. As the tribe numbers increased, it became more and more difficult to keep order amongst the members, so the leaders came up with the idea of reward and punishment. This system of control evolved into the religions we have today. If you are good, the all-seeing almighty God will reward you, and your place by His side in heaven will be assured; if you are bad and do not obey or respect the words of God, you will be punished for your disobedience and cast down to live in hell with Satan for the rest of eternity.

The religions upon the Earth today are still all about controlling others in an attempt to keep order amongst the masses. People are starting to lose their faith because the rewards that the religious leaders are promising can only be received when they are dead. Churches throughout the Western world are being closed down through lack of support, and religious orders have started to decline in popularity. There is a new method of control that has descended upon the world's population: governments. When politicians started to rule the world's countries, their goal was to keep control of the masses by keeping them poor and wanting, but there was no mention of God. The reward they offered the people for obeying the law was, and still is, staying out of prison.

I do think there is a place for religion in today's world, especially for those who can find solace within their faith and the belief that God is watching over them, but be careful: Maintaining a belief that is static and ignoring other methods of understanding will not move the believer forward. The universe is dynamic, as is everything around us on this world. New discoveries and new understandings appear around us every day. Do not get bogged down by the fog of belief, but learn to accept change. Believing, or having faith, is not 'knowing'. When one believes something is true or has faith that what one has been taught is right and true, that does not necessarily mean that these things are correct. It is not a question of establishing proof that something is right or wrong; the truth will always shine through. Be prepared to have your faith shaken, as not everything around us is always what it seems to be.

To recap something I mentioned in a previous chapter, we are too far down the ladder for God to influence our life. We are too remote from God to be able to comprehend who or what God is, and I doubt very much if God knows us personally, regardless of what our religious leaders teach us. God will be aware of our existence because there is always a beginning for new life to appear, but we are not yet evolved enough, nor have we developed a vibrational frequency high enough, to be at a compatible level for God to recognise us or for us to understand who God is.

We should be looking within ourselves for leadership and guidance from our higher self, our God. Our higher self is as close as we can get to a supreme being. We should recognise this and learn to listen for the help and guidance it sends us every day from within.

Our church is not a building we need to visit once a week in order to send our prayers. Our church is within us. We do not have to shout on high or display ourselves to others in order to show how holy we are. The God inside us is always listening, so just a quiet thought is all that is necessary. When you pray to or ask your higher self a question, if you are listening, you will always receive an answer. When you are able to understand that your higher self is *your* God, you will realise that your higher self is personal to you, and you do not have to share your God with anyone else. There is not a hundred million people praying and asking questions to your higher self; your higher self only hears you and only responds to you.

You are only here on this world because your higher self sent you here. It is your job to learn and experience the things that your higher self needs to know, as your higher self is unable to come to a world like this. There is no reason why your higher self should listen to anyone else, as your higher self only needs to know how you are getting on and whether you are having any problem with what you are learning or experiencing.

You have got 100 per cent attention from your higher self at all times. This is great news for you, as you do not have to compete with anyone else for the attention of God. When you truly believe that, it should inspire you to want to learn as much as you can, because when your higher self evolves and is able to move on, so are you. Living your life to the full will help you to learn quickly, as it has all the elements that you require to stay strong and healthy in both your mental attitude towards life and your physical ability to stay the course. This will give you a better chance to complete your life here without too much struggling.

## More on intuition

In today's world, there doesn't seem to be much time for intuition. Many people think that intuition is an ability that has been gifted to a chosen few, or that it is just an ability a few eccentric people profess to have but are unable to provide any evidence or actual proof of what they are seeing, hearing, or feeling. In today's busy world, there is too much noise, too much urgency, and very little patience. This highly competitive way of living compels people to rush around after others, leaving no time for themselves. Everything is needed yesterday or sooner; you must stop for a while to relax and listen. Unfortunately, taking a break these days means sitting outside the local coffee house and posing with a cappuccino and a blueberry muffin while gossiping with friends.

Have you noticed how loud everything seems to be? People are now talking at the top of their voices in order to be heard, so it is no wonder that few people can hear the voice inside. The sound of guidance has become so quiet that for most people, it is less than a whisper. Is it any wonder that intuition plays little or no part at all in most people's lives? Intuition is not a gift, it is a necessity. It is not something you need to provide proof of. Intuition is a very real ability that covers a wide range of senses within the body, and all you have to do is look, listen, feel, and have patience.

Although a large majority of people enjoy limited free will, and since this free will is not total, it is important that we are aware that there could be occasions when life becomes uncertain. Guidance may be needed to show us what to do next – or perhaps we may need help to show us the way back onto our path if we have inadvertently been led astray. Throughout our life on the Earth, various gifted people have elected to help us, should we need them. These people are called *guides*, and they work together with our higher self. They offer their specialist help freely to us, but only when it is needed.

They are not here to influence the path of our life in any way and will only intervene as a last resort. They are not Red Indian, Tibetan, Chinese, or highly intelligent New Age travelling guides. They are people who have already been through what we are going through now and have first-hand knowledge and experience to help others who are struggling.

These individuals no longer need to come back to this world, as they have already acquired the knowledge and wisdom that this system has given them. They have broken the cycle of birth and death but have elected to stay within this system, as it will be beneficial for them in the future if they stay here to pass on their knowledge to those who need it. There are also people who are living on this world in our lifetime who are here specifically to help others with their specialist knowledge. These people are also experienced guides and will come into our life when needed and leave when their work is done. We attract these people to us by our intuitive thoughts and the frequency of our vibrations, to help us get through difficult times when there are problems within our life.

How does intuition work? What do you have to do to be intuitive? Everyone is intuitive. What makes the difference between a person's intuitive abilities is their perception. To be aware at all times that help and guidance is always available to you when you need it will make the perception of your intuition stronger. If the voice in your head is less than a whisper, listen harder. If your intuitive messages come to you in the form of a vision or symbols, look harder. If you are a person who has intuitive feelings, be better aware of what your body is telling you. When you use your intuitive potential to its maximum, you will be making the most of the help and guidance that are available to you. You will be living your life to the full, and your lessons here should be learned quickly and with ease.

## Entities

Unfortunately, sometimes the voices inside your head or the things you are feeling are not helpful. You may be getting guidance from something other than your higher self. Sometimes you can become the victim of forces that are far from positive. On occasion, you can attract entities to yourself that cling to your body and affect the way that you think – especially, but not necessarily, if you work with energy.

It is always advisable to be protected when working with energy. Entities – and there are various varieties of them – are negative energy, and they can be picked up by anyone, especially if you are feeling a bit stressed or under the weather. They are attracted by the low vibration being emitted, and the effect that they have on their victims is quite varied.

I have been the victim of what can only be called an attack upon my mind that affected my actions and the things that were happening around me. It can be quite alarming when things start to go wrong – not just once but time after time. I went through a period of about three months when I thought that I was living a different life. I had a series of things happening to me that I couldn't explain. Nothing seemed to go right; whatever I touched or started would go wrong or break down. At first it was not alarming, as nothing lasts forever, but then something else would go wrong or break and somebody else would break something of mine. Projects that I planned to start would fail to materialise.

This went on for months, one thing after another. What seemed to magnify the problem was that I was going through a lean period financially, and the replacement cost for all of the breakages and the money spent on failed projects were building up. There were constant delays with events that were supposed to happen with no foreseen problems. Friends saw me as a different person. The more unhappy I became, the more things went wrong. This was a life-changing time. I felt powerless and unable to get myself back to normal. Fortunately, this period was only temporary as one of my friends recognised what was happening and put things right for me.

If you ever you find yourself in a similar situation, don't just put it down to bad luck. There is no such thing. Everything has a cause and an effect. Things don't just happen on their own, nor are they put right by a change of luck. It will require action from you to put things right, either by helping yourself or by seeking help from others.

## Key Points

It is important to understand that our life on Earth is only temporary. Our physical body has an allotted life span but we don't when our body dies we move on to where our higher self sends us.

Throughout the many lives we live, we cannot exist without help from our higher self. We need guidance from our higher self in order to know what to do next. Without guidance we would just drift around not knowing what to do. Our intuition connects us to our higher self so it is important to listen out for the information that will guide us through this and every life we live.

# Chapter 14

# For What Purpose?

Why should you go to all the effort of living your life to the full? If you have read everything in this book so far, you will know that there is quite lot of hassle involved. You will have to change your lifestyle, change what you eat, keep your body fit, keep your mind fit, and learn how to breathe and relax properly. There's a possibility that you may also be thinking, "Why should I change? I feel great as I am!" I can already hear you saying, "I've lived for many years without any problems, so why should I bother to change now?"

Well, I am here to tell you that there is a good reason why you should implement changes in your life and start living your life to the full. Everything in this universe has a purpose, even if it is not apparent. Let us look within our universe to see an example of what I mean.

For what purpose are there so many stars in our universe? I can't believe that they were put there just for our benefit or as something to give us a bit of light relief and gaze at when it gets dark. Unfortunately, because of our limited vision, we are only able see a very small selection of stars with the naked eye – maybe two or three hundred at best – and those stars visible to us are our very closest neighbours. Our galaxy, the Milky Way, has upwards of 200 trillion stars within it. Our universe also has upwards of 200,000 billion galaxies within it, so I think that we can safely say that they were not put there for our amusement. There must be another reason for their existence, because everything has a purpose.

It has come to light in recent years that our sun is not the only star in our galaxy that has planets in orbit around it. I suspect this will also be the case within every galaxy in the universe. So that begs the question: is there life in the universe besides our own? The answer is obvious: yes, of course there is. Even the narrowest-minded scientist, religious teacher, or power-hungry politician has to realise eventually that we are not alone. For what other purpose would a universe exist, if it were not to house life?

There are ninety-eight naturally occurring elements in the universe, and the purpose of these elements is to be the building blocks of a universe. A universe without anything in it is not a universe, it is a void. There are stars housed within every galaxy that are so massive and burn so hot and bright they could not possibly support life on any planets that may be in orbit around them. This type of star uses its fuel at a much quicker rate than a smaller, more stable star like our sun. A star of this type will have a much shorter life expectancy, because it will use up its fuel very quickly. Any life on a planet that may be in orbit around it would have to live in very extreme conditions and may not have enough time to evolve.

What is the purpose of a star like that? It seems an awful waste – creating a giant star that burns away too quickly to be of any use. But everything has a purpose, even a giant star.

This type of star, when it reaches the end of its life, grows even bigger. It does so when the hydrogen that it uses as fuel runs out. It is at this point that the star begins to use helium to fuel itself. Its colour changes to a deep red as it grows even bigger into what is called a *red giant*. Our sun can be dwarfed by a red giant star over a thousand times in size.

In time, the red giant, with most of its fuel depleted, begins to implode (the core of the star collapses in upon itself). The gravitational pressure that this star creates as it collapses is so immense that, when it reaches a critical point, the red giant explodes with such unimaginable force that it releases most of its energy at once. For a short while, it can become the brightest object in the galaxy where it was housed as it blows itself to bits. This explosion is called a *supernova*.

As the material of the exploding red giant is flung into space, it leaves behind an object which can be as small as ten miles across its diameter, spinning at an unimaginable speed. This is known as a *pulsar* (the most famous being housed in the Crab Nebula). If the exploding star is really massive, it may create a neutron star as it explodes; or, if the gravitational pull of the implosion is strong enough, a black hole will form.

As the material from the supernova spreads out into space, it takes with it all of the newly created heavy elements that were created during the massive explosion. These new elements will mingle with the gas and dust that has formed into a huge cloud called a *nebula*.

It has been known for a while that nebulae are the birthplaces of new stars and planets, like our own sun, the Earth, and the other seven planets within our solar system. The newly created heavy elements that can only have been created in the immense heat and pressure during the explosion of the supernova and sudden death of the red giant star will eventually come together with other materials – such as gases, dust, and rock that were also created from the explosion – to form many solar systems like the one that contains our sun, including the Earth and all of the other orbiting planets. We can recognise some of these newly created heavy elements from the supernova explosion, as they are here on Earth today in the form of gold, platinum, mercury, and lead. These elements could not have been created in any other way.

So you see, there is a purpose for everything, even if we are not smart enough to understand it. Nothing is wasted. There is also a purpose for living your life to the full.

If you have read this book carefully up to this point, you must have realised by now that to live your life to the full will take a little effort on your part. Just one step at a time is all that is needed to start the ball rolling; it will appear to be hard at the beginning because change is always difficult. There will always be the inevitable setbacks; just when you think you have cracked it, you'll realise you haven't. Successes are always hard-won until your body and mind can adjust to the changes.

Failures are just as important as successes, because you will always learn much more from adversity. There is always a purpose for everything that happens to you. Your successes and your failures are all a part of the learning curve, each one building you up and taking you one step nearer to your goal. So what is the prize? What is at the end of the long bouts of training and the numerous changes you will need to go through and the hardship you may have to endure? What makes this suffering worthwhile?

Suffering is what you may believe you are going though when you first start out on the journey to living your life to the full. After the first six months of maintaining this regime, and as your body starts to adjust to the changes that are happening inside you, you will find that you can and will want to do more. You are beginning to feel the difference within your body as it repairs itself and becomes stronger internally as well as externally.

The way your mind works will also be altered as it undergoes changes; it is now fully oxygenated and nourished with the extra chi. It is inevitable that once you realise the improvements that have been made to your health – because of the weight lost or weight gained to bring your body back into balance – and see just how different you are feeling physically and how clear your thoughts are, you will not want to return to the way you were. There is only one way you are going from now on, and that is forward. The further forward you go, the easier it will be for you to go further still. Living life to the full will do this for you

Being healthy makes you feel good and bright with no need for any trips to the doctor, no more prescriptions to pay for, and no need to take drugs or suffer side effects. Your body will heal itself easily and automatically, even before symptoms start to show. Treat your body right, and it will protect you from any illness no matter what it is called. If you keep your immune system strong, it will fight off any viral or bacterial attacks before they can gain a hold on you. Living your life to the full will do this for you.

If you are unlucky enough to have had an accident and that accident is not terminal, and if your body and mind are strong and healthy, then no matter what injury has been sustained, it will heal quickly and thoroughly irrespective of what age you are. Remember, age is not determined by how long you have been living on the Earth but by the condition of your body and mind. As a result of living your life to the full, you will suffer less over the recovery time from the injury because your body and mind are fully functional and there is nothing in the way to impede the healing process. If stress is a problem in your life, the healing process will take longer. It doesn't matter what other symptoms you have besides the injury you have sustained, these symptoms will all be stress-induced. For example, if you are overweight or underweight, or perhaps you are suffering with emotional problems such as anger, jealousy, egotism, and greed – in fact, if for any reason you are living outside of the parameters that have been set for you during your stay here – you will be suffering from stress and this will slow down the process of healing your injury.

On this world, it is all about the body. If you look after your body, you will find it easier to succeed while you are here. On the other hand, if you abuse your body, you will create more work and suffering for yourself. As mentioned before, your body is designed to last longer than the allotted time of your stay here. If you abuse your body and it dies before you are able to finish the lessons you came here to learn, you will have to return here again – not only to finish the lessons you were previously unable to learn, but also to learn and understand the reason for the premature death of your previous body, so that it doesn't happen again in any other lives you may have to live.

It is much easier to come here and get on with the task at hand. Listen to your higher self and any guides that have been assigned to help and guide you during your stay here. Do not let others influence you, as they do not have the qualifications to do so, nor do they have any idea what lessons you are here to learn. How could they have any idea? Most people are unaware why they are here themselves. They don't know because this knowledge is stored within the subconscious area of their mind, and it is only released in small pieces when it is relevant and ready to be used. So how could anybody know what lessons you have or for what reason you have come to this world?

It also goes without saying – but I will say it anyway – that this also applies to you. If you influence others by persuading them to do what you think is right for them, be prepared to accept the consequence of any karmic action that may be bestowed upon you as a result of your interference.

It is surprising how many people come to this world with an attitude. They come here mostly to do what they want and have a good time and there is nothing wrong with that, except that they forget the main reason for coming to the Earth. Nobody can drop out or evade responsibility. We have plenty of time to learn our lessons, with more than enough time to experience the pleasure of life.

Keeping yourself on the right path is as much your responsibility as it is that of your higher self. If you are not listening to your higher self, you cannot be guided; if your physical and mental faculties are not functioning properly, your body may not last the distance. Keeping your mind functioning properly and your body in good running order is one of the main tasks assigned to you during your stay upon this world. Living your life to the full will help you to do just that. Being able to accomplish what you set out to do when you arrived here and carrying out the tasks as they are presented to you in the easiest and most efficient way is the prize. Living your life to the full can help you stay the course and enable you to achieve all your goals at this visit easily, even with enough time to experience the pleasures of life on this world.

It is for this purpose you have come to this world.

## Second-hand knowledge

During my early years upon the Earth, I lacked understanding and knew very little about the purpose of my life. Why this was a concern to me at such a young age, I'll never know. Anyway, the struggle lasted for a number of years, until through the guidance of my higher self I turned to religion to find the answer. I was born a Church of England Christian, so I started there. I attended my local church every week but soon realised that their teachings were not answering my questions.

In those days, every churchgoer was taught to be God-fearing. In order to be accepted into heaven by the Lord, Christians were expected to go out of their way to forgive and care for others and perform only good deeds whilst expounding the word of God. Failure to comply with this teaching would cast your soul to the devil, and you would burn in hell for eternity (or until the fuel ran out!). One thing that used to puzzle me was that most people didn't go to church, and they didn't seem to care about whether they were going burn in hell or not.

My life as a God-fearing Christian lasted a few years, until I realised that Christianity was unable to fulfil my thirst for knowledge. I decided to look elsewhere and drifted from one thing to another until I discovered Buddhism. Buddhists were saying much the same things as Christians, except that they wrapped their word differently. They also taught their followers not to be too good or too bad but to take the middle way. This, I discovered, was sound advice that has stood me in good stead throughout my life. Another positive thing to come out of my Buddhist experience was the introduction to meditation, which I still practice today.

Unfortunately, Buddhist teachings also avoided the question "What is the purpose of life upon Earth?" If God created everything and these religious leaders were teaching the word of God, then surely he must have told them what our purpose for life upon the Earth is and directed them to pass on this teaching to everyone. It was not enough to say you must be kind and thoughtful towards others, and if you sin don't sin too much. It took me quite a while to realise that the reason they were not teaching the purpose of life on Earth is because they didn't know. I also know now that what they were teaching had very little to do with God but a great deal to do with the politics of the day, and that their only interest was to further their own influence over others to maintain their wealth and power.

It came as a bit of a shock when I finally realised that no one knew the purpose of life upon the Earth, and an even bigger shock when I understood what religion was really all about. It was about control: control of the masses by fear. In today's world, religious orders have relinquished most of their power to politicians and the wealthier amongst us, many of whom have little moral fibre or religious scruples. God help us all for the future. I quote the words of Wallace D Wattles: "God has worked a long time and very patiently to bring us where we are in industry and government; and he is going right on with his work. I believe that he will do away with Plutocrats, trust magnates, captains of industry and politicians, as soon as they

can be spared but in the meantime they are very necessary."
I can't wait!!

For many years, I contemplated the question, "For what purpose is there life on Earth?" but the answer eluded me and everyone else, it seemed. Then gradually, through reading, meditation, and pondering the subject, I realised that God, as we have been taught to know him, does not exist. Please don't misunderstand me – I am not saying that God does not exist. I am saying that how we have been taught to recognise God is wrong. God is within us, and we are a part of God. Our God is our higher self.

Once I knew this, the purpose of our life upon Earth gradually became apparent. Everything we need to know on a personal level comes to our conscious mind from our higher self via our subconscious mind. I want to make it perfectly clear exactly what I am saying here. Everything that has ever been taught to us about religion, politics, the power that mankind should have, and even how people are expected to behave within society – everything that we know to this date that affects everybody on this planet – has always been handed down from one human being to another human being until it has now finally reached us, and that is the complete sum of all *human* knowledge. It is not first-hand knowledge.

Every single scrap of human knowledge that we know today is open for debate as to its accuracy. Just look at the way the politicians of today change, twist, or manipulate information to suit their own ends. What is to say that the knowledge that has been handed down to us for hundreds of thousands of years has not already been altered, manipulated, or even excluded from the knowledge banks altogether to keep it a secret from us? There is only one way to ensure that the knowledge you are getting now is true first-hand knowledge, and that is to get this knowledge straight from your higher self.

It was by asking the question to my higher self that I came to understand the purpose of life upon the Earth, which I believe was excluded from the teachings that had been handed down previously to me. Don't take my word for it; ask your own questions, and you will be amazed how inaccurate the history of mankind is and how much has been kept secret from us to keep the power and wealth where it is today.

## It's all about the body

As I have mentioned previously, this life is all about the body. Living your life to the full is about looking after your body. While you are living on this world, your body and mind are the most important allies you have, so keeping command over them both should be your first priority. There are other tools which have been loaned to you for the duration of your stay upon the Earth, but without your body and mind, it would be impossible to complete the lessons and tasks you came here for. In fact, without them, it is not possible for you to come here at all. Your physical body operates at the same frequency as this world and is designed to work naturally upon the Earth; it cannot exist anywhere else unaided. You, on the other hand – the real you – vibrate at a much higher frequency.

If you tried to come to the Earth without the aid of the human body around you, then you would drift right through it as if you were not here. This is because the molecular structure of your real body is more widely dispersed and vibrates at a much faster rate than that of the Earth and the physical human body that it is occupying. Your human body has been designed to accept and be compatible with your real body. This is made possible by increasing the speed of its internal frequency so that it vibrates within the parameters of its host; it will then act as an anchor and hold the host in place when it has taken possession.

The human body operates using bioelectricity, and if the human body is abused by its host, the electrical current that flows through it can alter and affect the internal organs and may also affect the way the brain operates. If the human body becomes unbalanced enough to affect the bioelectrical flow within it through continual abuse, the stress caused to the internal organs may have a detrimental effect on their longevity.

What kind of abuse are we referring to? Well, I know that it is hard to say no to that juicy steak and chips with all the trimmings, and I know that it is hard to say no to that bottle of beer which is going to help you forget your troubles for a while. I also realise that a glass of water just doesn't have that same appeal – and why should you say no to that cigarette when your body craves its hourly shot of nicotine? I also understand that processed ready meals are slightly cheaper than fresh food and quicker to prepare. If they are eaten frequently, however, they may turn out to be more expensive in the long run.

If you put cheaper low-grade fuel in your car it will not run properly; this is also the case with the human body. It doesn't matter so much with a car, as it is not a matter of life and death if your car doesn't start one day; it will just cause a little inconvenience. On the other hand, it might be a little more serious if your body decided not to start one day. To prevent this from happening, right now would be a good time to check on how you are treating your body.

So what do you need to check? Most people live their lives without a second thought as to how they are living. Their particular routine is normal to them. If they feel comfortable living as they do, then why should they check on how they are living? It may not be something that would even cross their mind. Personally, I believe it is a good thing to check and see how your body is doing every once in a while. Let's see what we need to look at.

First, consider your weight. Are you overweight or underweight? Either way, your body is out of balance. If you think that this applies to you, take a look at your diet. Do you have a balanced diet? When you eat the correct food, you will lose weight if you need to or gain weight if you need to.

In addition to checking your diet, consider the amount of exercise you are doing. If you are overweight, the correct exercises for you to undertake are stretching and muscle-strengthening so that as you lose the extra weight you have been carrying around, your skin will maintain its elasticity and will not hang down your body, and your muscles will become stronger and not waste away. If you are underweight, the same exercises apply, as your muscles will need to be stronger if you are to carry more weight around than you are used to, and your skin needs to become more pliable to enable it to stretch when you put on those extra few pounds your body needs. Qigong and t'ai chi are excellent forms of exercise that will enable you to achieve this gently without the grunting and groaning you may need to do with other forms of exercise.

In terms of your general health, do you find that you are visiting the doctor or the hospital a little more often than you would really like to? Or maybe you've started to puff and blow more when walking – or perhaps there are activities that you found easy to do a few years ago but now require a lot more effort to perform? Perhaps it's time to take a look at your lifestyle. When you are young – let's say from your late teens to your late thirties – the punishment you put your body through could, within reason, easily be absorbed or shrugged off; but as you get older, your body can't handle the same sort of treatment and remain unscathed. The recovery time between each event becomes longer because the quantity of healing chi within the body diminishes with age.

## So what is the solution?

In a previous chapter, I explained about ageing within the body and mind. Your age is not determined by how long you have lived on the Earth but by the condition of your mind and your physical body. This is good news if you are getting on in years, because it means that you can do something about it. You can recover some of the youthfulness you have lost over the years by changing your lifestyle and increasing the diminished chi within your body. There is no need to continue to live out the false belief that, when you are on the slippery road that leads to your death, you need to become old first to get there. I intend to remain young, fit, and healthy right up to the moment it is time for me to leave, and you are in a position to do that too.

Living your life to the full will benefit you by increasing the chi within your body. This will help you to heal more quickly and keep your body from being susceptible to the continuous bouts of illness that ageing brings. It does this by keeping your cells from acting old. Your skin remains soft and pliable, and your internal organs stay healthy and continue to operate properly. Your mind maintains its clarity of thought and gives you not only a better chance to consciously enjoy the life you have but also the ability to solve everyday problems by having the advantage of focused thought acquired from the practise of meditation.

It will not give you increased longevity, because at this stage of your existence the lessons that you are learning here now do not require any more time than you have already been given. But because your health and general well-being have improved since you began to live your life to the full, your body will last you comfortably right up until the day you die.

I am not passing on this message in book form so that I can make a fortune from everyone who lives life to the full. I get no money apart from a percentage of the sale of this book. There is no "Life to the Full" kit that you can buy from me that will keep you fit and healthy and make me rich. I am expounding the virtues within this book because people should know that there is an alternative available to them besides what is on offer at the moment, and what is on offer at the moment is really not that good. There is one thing certain that needs no more proof than looking around and seeing the evidence before your very eyes yourself.

The system that is in place now just does not work, especially for the ordinary person in the street, and it only appears to be working for those who are wealthy and in power because they are able to cover up the cracks. The system in use today is no longer sustainable, and this will become apparent over the coming years.

There are many campaigns running at the moment to try to save the world. It is not the world that needs saving; the world can look after itself. No matter what we do to it, it will always recover. It is the human race that needs saving. We will become the endangered species if we continue to live as we are at the moment.

This can change, and you can make these changes happen by implementing the suggestions in this book. Show others the truth by living your life to the full and leading by example. Do not rely on others to save you from the inevitable changes that are upon us; they will not be there when you need them. They will become like you are now – lost and drifting through life, just another part of the system. Begin now to live your life to the full, and it will set you apart from others and release you from the system you are being forced to live in. When politicians and plutocrats of the day have no more answers and the system begins to crash, your mind will be strong and clear. Who knows – it could be you they will call upon to find the answers.

When our leaders, along with a large portion of the population, are weakened by the continuous consumption of poisoned addictive food, they will begin to falter because their body and mind cannot work properly. When, because of a lack of the correct exercise, correct breathing, and focused thought, they find it a struggle to put this world back on track, you will be ready to step in and rebuild, thanks to the changes you have gone through and a lifestyle that makes you strong inside and out.

When you are practising the correct exercise, you will notice how much fitter you are compared to those people around you, and your confidence will set you apart from others. When the majority are ill and suffering from the side effects brought about by prescribed drugs that are no longer able to heal, you will be fit and healthy with no need for medication. You will know how to save yourself and others when the time is ready – and make no mistake, change is at hand.

This may sound a little dramatic and would probably make a good script for a film, but unfortunately, this life drama is real. People are ill for much of their life – not necessarily seriously ill, but ill enough to make a difference to their life.

There are a large number of people who have become extremely overweight and addicted to the food they eat. The food is processed and has been made to eat straight away or maybe warmed up in a microwave oven. This type of food has addictive ingredients and artificial additives purposely included so that the people who consume it will enjoy its taste so much that they will feel compelled to buy the product again. This is not fiction, and it tells you something about the morality of the people who make it.

Money is printed at will with nothing of wealth to back it up. This creates a false economy which is unsustainable over the long term. Any economy must have the backing of real wealth behind it if it is to be able to pay its way. Crime rates throughout the world are increasing dramatically, with little evidence that anybody can do much about it. I have mentioned other social problems in this book, but the list goes on. Change is at hand, and it should be embraced by everyone. For many, however, change can be difficult to handle. There is a saying that people refer to when they are uncertain of the outcome when change is happening: "Better the devil you know." I am not sure that it is better to keep the devil we have now.

We are living in the age of competition, where people have to fight for their fair share of the available wealth on this world. This system creates a false impression that there is a lack of abundance. When companies or individuals need to compete against each other for something they want, they are doing so because they think that there is a shortage of whatever they need. That is why they are competing.

This shortage may appear to be real in the competitive world, but outside of the competitive world there is an abundance of everything you could ever want. Competition creates greed, aggression, egotism, and poverty. Live your life to the full and live where the abundance is, in the creative world.

You'll see the bigger picture in the next chapter.

## Key points

There is always a purpose for the things that happen to us as we go through life whether we understand them or not. Nothing is left to chance. We may not understand what is going on because of our lack of knowledge, or our inability or recognise the reason why things happen, but there is defiantly a purpose for living life to the full. It just needs a little effort on your part and you will start to enjoy the benefits.

Do not settle for second hand knowledge it may not be reliable and could well be manipulative. Ask the question to your higher self and you will always receive an answer and it will always be the truth.

It is all about the body on this world, your body is the tool that has been loaned to us for our stay here, it will enable us to learn and complete the lessons for our higher self. If we abuse our body and it dies before we are able to complete our lessons, we will have to return to this world again to complete them. To keep your body in tip top condition so that it can stay the course, live your life to the full.

# Chapter 15

# We Can Make Changes

If the people of each nation throughout the whole world would come together as a single collective mind and consider the proposals I am now putting forward, the Earth as we know it would end, and through the single-minded focused thought of all people, a new Earth would be born. The birth of the new Earth would be such that its status would be raised to that of a paradise, or as close to a paradise as could be achieved in this universe.

To implement such changes will not be easy. The first thing we must do before progress can be made is to help each person think in a positive and productive way that would be for everyone's benefit, not just the individual's. I am not suggesting that everybody should be brainwashed to accept the new changes unconditionally. Far from it – change must come naturally and without force. Let's look at what people throughout the world generally think about, and we will see what pitfalls we are likely to encounter. We can then make some useful suggestions that, when put forward, will express the benefits everyone will receive when these changes come to fruition.

For the changes I am suggesting to work, they must be introduced to everybody in each nation throughout the world. Everybody must be in agreement with the general direction that our world should be heading. These changes will affect everyone, so there can be no exceptions. There must be total acceptance from every nation. In order to get overall acceptance, it is important that everyone understand that the world they are living on now is run by a minority of people who are able to manipulate the majority through wealth and power. To make this a fairer world for everybody, this must change.

In order for changes to take place, everyone must understand that our possessions, no matter how expensive or numerous, do not actually belong to us. We entered this world with no material wealth or possessions, and we will leave this world exactly the same way. Everything we believe belongs to us during our stay here is not actually ours; it is only on loan to us for the duration of our stay. Once this fact is fully understood and accepted, we will have jumped the first hurdle.

It may be harder for those of wealth and power to grasp this concept with an open heart, as they will believe that they have the most to give up, but this is not the case. Nobody is giving up anything because nobody owns anything. In the new world, certain things will no longer be necessary, and these will be discarded. New things will replace the old.

## The abolition of money

Money may not be at the top of everybody's list as the one thing that is essential to have in life, but it will be fairly high up on most people's, because having lots of money in an economy-based society gives one power, security, and opportunities that a person without money will never have. Money must be dispensed with in favour of a different system.

I have given a great deal of thought as to what other Items need to be discarded along with money, but I really couldn't think of anything else. Dispensing with money seems to do the trick. How can this be? How is it possible that taking one item out of the equation can solve almost all other problems? In an economy-based society, money is king. It has so much influence and so much power attached to it that it affects pretty much everything. When such importance is attached to one thing, it is easy to see how too much power corrupts.

When money is finally dispensed with, there are two ways we can go. The first is to carry on as we are but without money. This could present problems. Chaos would descend on the populations of all nations, wreaking havoc throughout the world. Individuals would have to fend for themselves, using whatever possessions they have as barter for the essential things they may need. It will be the strong against the weak and the survival of the fittest. The ruthless will rule the world, as they are strong and able to take whatever they want from whoever they want. The weak will become their slaves.

This is a frightening prospect, and clearly one without much potential. Societies and civilizations cannot survive without a stable structure and order. Resentment will arise amongst people who are enslaved, and the only course of action they can take is to become stronger and eventually overthrow their ruthless rulers. A cycle will be created as rulers are overthrown by their slaves and become slaves themselves. They then grow stronger again and overthrow their rulers. This is likely to continue for a while until something more positive happens, like perhaps the arrival of a world leader, a saviour, someone who has skills in this field from a previous life experience who has been sent here to guide the world's population to a more stable existence.

The second way to handle the elimination of money is for everyone to learn to work together for each other. We all will have to do our bit for the good of humanity and all things will become equal for everyone. Can you imagine that? I know that this is a completely different concept and one that has never been tried before. It is totally opposite from the way we are living now. Everybody would have equal wealth and power without the need for money.

At first glance, it may appear that I am suggesting a worldwide communist state, but all existing communist countries have wealthy and powerful leaders who try to keep the masses equal amongst themselves but still under the leaders' control. This system may work well for the leaders and those who have found wealth and power within that system, but ordinary people are still repressed. These are exactly the same problems that are present in a capitalist system, and that is because both of these societies are economy-based. In fact, every country has an economy-based society, no matter what brand of politics it claims. Take money out of the equation, and we could start afresh.

There would have to be some radical changes in the way that people think. We must eliminate the "fight to be right" attitude of the ego and stay within the parameters set for us by expressing our belief of what is best for everyone. Instead of all for one, it would need to be one for all. Everybody would have to learn how to conquer negative emotions and eliminate such things as greed, envy, anger, hatred, violence, and egotistic tendencies. I understand that this will not happen overnight, and I realise that even making a start to rid ourselves of these vices would be a monumental task, but the eventual outcome would benefit everyone, the rewards would be enormous, and we would all be life rich.

Let us look at what will be gained from our newfound freedom from financial stress. First of all, imagine everybody working together and contributing technical skills openly. The technological advancement made in the first few years would be enormous – but beyond that, we can only provide a rough guess as to what our achievements would be. There would be no competition amongst large corporations, as there wouldn't *be* any large corporations. Scientists would work together, as would the whole workforce. Without the need for competition and the greed that is manifested alongside it, we would be left with only creativity. Everybody would be able to play his or her part, as unemployment would no longer exist.

Every job within each community would be placed at the same value. A road sweeper's job would be placed at the same value as that of a doctor or a scientist, and as there would be no payment for any of the work involved, every job would be deemed as important for the community as any other job. All work would be performed for the good of mankind as a whole and in turn would greatly benefit each individual person in every country throughout the world.

As technology throughout the world advanced, machines would do the more manual tasks, freeing up people to learn new skills. But it is not just about work – it is also about living a happy and worthwhile life. Everyone would still have a path to follow, as this is the main reason for coming to this world in the first place. There would still be as many challenges as there are now.

Medical science would advance much faster than it does today as a result of scientists sharing their work and ideas freely. The time would soon come when they are able to develop real remedies that actually work on the underlying cause of an illness, instead of developing profit-making drugs that only alleviate the symptoms. There should no longer be any reason for researchers to direct their energy into making a profit, as the work they are doing will only be done for the good of everybody. When financial pressure is taken away, there would be no need to build up the bank balance to satisfy shareholders.

Eventually, a large medical industry will no longer be needed and could be reduced in size considerably to care only for those who have accidents. There should be a sharp drop in the number of cases of illness when it is realised that prevention is better than a cure, and more effort would go into educating people to prevent illness from happening altogether.

The police forces all over the world could be scaled down or in some cases even disbanded altogether, as they would no longer be needed to fight crime. With the elimination of money, greed would no longer be an issue, and many of the crimes we are seeing today wouldn't exist anymore because everything would be free anyway.

The abolition of money would change the thought processes within many people. In the present day, the definition of life generally leans towards negativity. Negative thoughts and emotions seem to be more prevalent now than ever before, but with the absence of money and the problems associated with it, the direction of thought would lean more to the positive side. Positive thoughts and emotions are more infectious than negative thoughts and emotions, so when the populations of the world have been infected with positivity, life on this world could for the most part be lived in relative harmony.

## Redundant professions

I shall mention here some of the professions that will no longer be needed when money is abolished, releasing employees to be retrained and learn skills that are more worthwhile and benefit everyone.

Advertising would be one of the first industries to be axed, as there would be no reason for companies to advertise something that is available to everyone for free. Banking would also go, along with all associated products and staff. There would no longer be any need for investors except to invest their time and effort by helping others instead of themselves. Moneylenders, who operate within the security of the financial services industry, would no longer be able to steal from the desperate or the gullible. These people can be retrained to genuinely help those in need without the sting in the tail after they have finished.

Stockbrokers and solicitors/lawyers, with all associated products and staff, would no longer be needed either. Insurance agents and politicians could all be made redundant, as these are throwaway professions that needed to be invented because of the presence of money. There are many other professions that could be dispensed with, as they will not be necessary when the world moves away from an economy-based society.

Politics as we know it today would cease to exist. Politicians all over the world, who are actually employed by us to look after the financial welfare and control of people within their countries, would no longer be needed. Instead, representatives from every country would be engaged to oversee the developments and improvements happening in their area and also to liaise with their counterparts throughout the world. The work they do would be placed at the same value as every other job and would not be regarded a position of power. Representatives would be changed frequently so there would be no room for power-hungry people to abuse their authority over others with thoughts of ruling the world.

When the amount of energy that is being used today and which has already been used in the past to fight for this, that, and everything else is taken into account, it is easy to see that living in a financially competitive world is just too expensive and really does not work. There should be no need to fight for the essentials in life as we are doing today. These things should be provided by the authorities we have already paid to provide them. It is all very well for them to say that they have run out of money, but they don't appear to be under any obligation to explain in plain English where the money has gone. When the world finally moves away from an economy-based society, there will be no need to fight for anything ever again. The energy that is being wasted on lost causes today can be used for a number of beneficial things.

One very worthy use would be to give our children a more thorough education. This would help them to fit into and become valued members of society, instead of rebelling and fighting against it. Teachers would be able to devote 100 per cent of their teaching time to their students without the need to worry about cutbacks, wage rises, and failing pension plans. Let us give the future generations of Earth a chance to do what we are failing to do right now.

## Modify the way we work

The system in use here today is one that has several companies within the same industry all making the same or very similar products. All are striving for the same goal, which is to be the market leader with their own products and to have their own brand name up in lights advertising the wonders of these products. Has it ever occurred to anyone that this is a little strange? Why should there be several different versions of the same product of varying quality and price on the market?

If every company were to merge into one manufacturer, with the design team and production staff from each company working together, pooling ideas, and manufacturing techniques to produce only one design of each product – which would be at the cutting edge of technology and manufactured to the highest standard possible to produce the very best quality – every product made would be the most technically advanced product possible at the time of manufacturing whilst also having the potential for a longer product lifespan. Adopting this system would use only a fraction of the resources that are being used in today's present system of cut-throat competition. Working in this way makes much more sense, and it could easily be achieved when money is taken out of the equation.

When we are able to eliminate the negative thought patterns that have been adopted over the past years, and we are able change our mindset to a more positive line of thought, perhaps we will be less concerned with how other people see us. It shouldn't matter how many possessions we have or whether our possessions are of a better quality or more expensive than others. The egotistic mindset that we seem to possess at the present time gives us a false sense of grandeur. Image is everything: "Look at me with my big house, my new car, the latest computer and TV." Image only appears to be important; it actually isn't. It is driven by the ego, a negative emotion that dictates how we should live our life. An ego-driven life is a life that insists we must always strive for the best no matter what the cost, just to look better than everybody else. Get rid of the ego. It won't be needed when money is abolished, because everybody can enjoy the best of everything all of the time.

With the formation of a financially free world, our lives will not alter too dramatically at first. We will still need to go to work, do the weekly shop, maintain our homes, and generally carry on with the mundane things that we have always done. But as technical advancements progress, we will enter a new age, one of creativity and enlightenment, that will bring peace and understanding to us all. We could then begin to help and care more for each other. It is at this point in our lives that we should adopt many of the components that would help us to live our life to the full.

## How on earth can we survive without money?

To many, life without money would be unthinkable. "How are we going to pay for the things we need?" "Does this mean that we will not get paid for the work we do?" "I don't get paid enough as it is. I really don't want to work for nothing." There are hundreds of other reasons that are totally understandable, but just like these few examples, they are all based on fear.

Do I think that creative living will happen soon? No, not in a million years! First we have to persuade the greedy, selfish, and power-hungry to relinquish their money, possessions, and power – even though in reality, they are not powerful and they own nothing. When they leave here, they will only able to take what they have learned and nothing else. Everything else is on loan. Even your husband or wife, your children, your relatives, and your friends are on loan. When you leave here, you go alone. Everything and everyone else stays.

It is my belief that, even if we all knew that the creative way of living was in the best interest of everyone, a far better way to live our lives, and a certain way to bring everybody wealth beyond their wildest dreams, it would still come down to the same old scenario. We would wait to see who was willing to go first – who was prepared to give up everything first. Until we get beyond this stumbling block, I am afraid that I cannot see just how this is going to happen.

A major event will have to occur to get the ball rolling – not necessarily something catastrophic, but something that will capture the human heart and change the way we are currently thinking. Perhaps it will take the arrival on Earth of someone who has the skills to lead us through the beginning stages of the creative way, someone who will help us recognise that all people, whatever their station in life, are equally important. We are all here for the same reason, and that is to strive to learn lessons that were set out for each of us and which represent our purpose for being on this world. We need guidance to help us realise what the truth is and take us along the path that will bring about the abolition of money and transport us to a better, more secure path than the one we are presently on.

## Key points

With the abolition of money and the breakup of the economy based society we live in now. Our attention can turn to a society of creative thinking people who will raise the status of this world and the advancement of themselves.

It will take courage and strength from the people of the Earth to see this through but the benefits gained will be worth it.

# Chapter 16

# The Way It Works

The creative system relies on all of us altering the way we think just a little – and I am referring here to the surrender of negative thoughts and emotions in favour of positive ones. We need, for example, to rid our minds of greed, anger, hate, jealousy, egotism, and selfishness. This type of emotional thinking must go. When our positive thoughts shine through, the way we perceive life on this world can change and bring with it the realisation that it doesn't have to be like this. Every one of us has the ability to change the way he or she is living right now.

We all have the skills required to create a new reality for ourselves – a reality that will elevate us above the need for money and the materialistic trappings of the life we are living at the moment. If we can leave the competitive way of life behind us with all the problems that it carries, we can live in paradise, or at least on a world that is substantially better than the present one. It is people who make this world what it is, and what we have at the moment is of our own making. Just a very small change in perception is all that is needed to improve living conditions on this world. Unfortunately, this will be, I believe, the stumbling block that may prevent the creative way of living from happening.

## The competitive way of life

The creative way of living is the opposite of the competitive way of life. The pressures placed upon people living in the competitive system, compels them to make as much money as they possibly can. The competition to do this is intense, and people who are unable to compete on this level – and this seems to be the majority – find themselves in a situation where their opportunities are limited and their way of life is difficult. Without enough money, there are limitations on what food they can buy, the kind of clothes they can afford, what type of housing they are able to live in, the type of car they drive, and so on.

In a creative world, perception of life is very different. There is no urgency to earn money and no urgency to accumulate material possessions; but having said that, however, nobody goes without. The need to acquire money in the competitive world is so great that companies will resort to all kinds of devious methods to win a sale. One such method that stands out at the moment is a trend that has developed which I find quite disturbing – where a company that advertises goods or services on TV, radio, or the Internet rubbish their main competitor in public at the same time.

There are other ways of making money for the chosen few. The lottery is a good example. With government approval, a company is selected to run the national lottery. This is tantamount to printing money for itself by relying on the desires and dreams of people who would like to better themselves by becoming rich. It is a captive market, because this is the desire and dream of most people.

It is a win-win situation for the government and the selected lottery company. A few people each week do become wealthier, and some of the money from the lottery does go to good causes, which places the government in a good light – but, the company that runs the lottery gets to keep a substantial percentage for itself, and the government also get its share from the income tax the company has to pay from those substantial profits.

This is how the competitive system works. A few people get the lion's share of the wealth and power (which is all they believe is available to them), while the majority of people work hard for the wealthy and powerful for very little reward (which is all they believe is available to them). At the time of writing, from the meagre wage that the majority of people earn, 20 per cent is spirited away before it is even received under the guise of income tax. If you are fortunate enough to be in a slightly higher-paid job, 40 per cent is taken from your wage. Then a further 20 per cent is taken every time you buy something, unless it is fuel for the car, cigarettes, alcohol, or any other so-called luxury item – and then the sky's the limit. This method taxing is called VAT; everybody just goes with it as if it's a normal part of life, but the government are actually taxing people twice. The majority of people are deliberately kept poor by the wealthy and powerful. The less fortunate can only watch in awe and dream as their peers celebrate their good fortune.

The above is an example of the visible competitive-thinking world. Even though there is more than enough for every single person on this world, this is seen as a lack by most people because the majority of the abundance is divided amongst the minority. This cannot happen in the invisible creative-thinking world, where the available resources are truly unlimited and available for everyone. They are just accessed in a different way.

## The creative way of life

The creative way of life is a much fairer way of living, as it gives everybody equal status. As mentioned before, two efforts will need to be undertaken before the creative system can be put into operation. The first is the worldwide abolition of the monetary system. The second and most important is the education that will introduce everyone to a different perception of life. You will be aware of this perception when you can change the way you think.

This is not a brainwashing exercise but the chance for everybody to understand that the life being lived now is not set in concrete; the circumstances of the life you are living now are not beyond your control to change; and there are many other options available. Provided the changes that you make to the life you want to live do not interfere with the lessons you have come here to learn, you could be anyone you want and do anything you want.

It is possible to educate people to dispense with their negative thought patterns and the attitude of want, want, want, and gain a more peaceful attitude of acceptance and gratitude for what they already have. This in turn will pave the way for a greater understanding and willingness to give freely of time and skills for the betterment of mankind. When the population of the world is able to work together by pooling skills and wisdom, the human race will progress much more quickly with technological and spiritual advancement. If we all could curb our enthusiasm in the quest to always be right and accept the possibility that others are also right, this will be a step in the right direction towards living in a creative world. When the ego is dispensed with and people are not too proud to accept the teachings and wisdom of others, the people on this world will be ready to move on to a brighter future.

I have already talked about some of the benefits and changes we will have after money has been dispensed with, but here we can go into the workings of a creative life in a little more detail. I believe that this proposal in general is sound, but I can also see that many people will think it unworkable. I can only give a general outline of its workings, which will leave many things to be discussed by people with far greater skills in this field than I possess. Anyway, let's see what we can do.

Apart from the abolition of money and the changes to people's general thought patterns, a list of basic requirements that people need to have to live a "normal life" would have to be drawn up to ensure that nobody goes short of items such as food, clothing, and housing. As every country has its own specific needs, this operation would be done by each country for its own people. At the beginning, everybody would collect or have delivered their food and general goods from the supermarket and the shops they would normally buy from – only now, no money would change hands. Shopping could eventually be done online, as some of it already is, and the need for the shopping experience we have today would dwindle as the retail trades changed from shops to automated warehouses for ease of distribution.

It should be made clear that every item a person or family receives which is essential to personal well-being and enables a comfortable and normal life should not be regarded as a free gift. Everyone must play his or her part by offering their skills, time, and commitment for the benefit of their community. The road sweepers would still sweep the roads, bakers would still bake, builders would continue to build, and trains would still transport people and goods, as would planes and ships. Every trade and service would continue to operate normally for the benefit of the whole community and would be placed at the same value and importance. The goods produced and the services provided would be operated by the people for the people and would benefit all mankind. There would be no need for anyone to go without.

This may seem at first sight a little unfair, if you compare the work that goes into building a house and the work that goes into baking a loaf of bread, but it all works out over a lifetime. If it takes a year for a hundred builders to build a housing estate, they are going to need to be fed and clothed not only for that year but for the rest of their lives. They will need tools and building materials to work with in order to do their job. They will also need transport to get to and from their job.

Although it is only going to take them a year to build the housing estate, they and their families will probably want to eat bread as well as other foods, and also be clothed, for the rest of their lives. How many meals and sets of clothes do you think that is for a hundred builders and their families? That is for the rest of their life, not just one year. Over a lifetime, it will all balance out. It is only when you introduce money into the equation that it goes wrong.

There are many people who think that their job and their efforts are more valuable than the effort that others put into their work. They also feel that they deserve to be paid more money just to do their job. This is arrogance and an egotistic way of thinking, as all work is done for the benefit of every human. When money comes into the equation, many feel that their contribution should be rewarded with a larger pay packet, but on this world everyone is here for the same reason, and that is to learn. No matter what your station in life, no one person is more valuable than any other. Get rid of the ego and understand that every one of us is equally valuable.

Delusions of grandeur must become a thing of the past if humanity is to move on. Everybody's worth must be recognised and cultivated by education. When the populations of all countries are provided with the appropriate education – not just the basics – then every nation can expect to see the benefits filter through their society within a very short time.

The educational system of the present day abandons many of its students, leaving them to fend for themselves when their basic education ends. This is the nature of a competitive and incomplete curriculum. Many young adults have no career path to follow when their basic education finishes; they are let loose in society to fend for themselves. Without guidance, they drift from job to job, not knowing what they want to do or be. For some, this can carry on until they are in their late thirties and forties. This is a waste of valuable talent. These individuals could be helping their communities and enjoying a full life.

The alternative is to increase the subjects on the school curriculum to include lessons like discovering your abilities, learning how to like yourself, and recognising your self-worth. Students could learn how to work with and help others to achieve. Young adults should be taught that every job has equal value and should therefore hold the same status. Its importance should not be measured by how much money you can get from performing it but by its usefulness to the community. In a world that has relinquished all of its ties with money, you would not be working just for yourself; you would be working for the good of everybody. Everybody should benefit from your efforts, and you should benefit from the efforts of other people also.

When education is not governed by money, other opportunities will surface. You may be able to take advantage of this by continuing your education while still working. This should bring enormous benefit to yourself and to those who, through your efforts of continued education, you are able to help.

When our young people begin to understand that working with others is important and that they should share ideas without expecting to gain from them, the world will be able to advance beyond its present status. Pooling knowledge will speed up our spiritual and technological advancement, taking us up to another level. Keeping your knowledge and ideas to yourself for profit will keep the world exactly where it is now and may be the catalyst for changes that will initiate the demise of the human race.

Future events are not a certainty. The future has not yet arrived, so any plans made in the present times for the future are just probabilities. They may or may not happen. The future has no power and can be changed before it becomes the present, so there is still time to stop the changes that have already been planned for this world and which will change the status of the Earth forever.

In order to stop the annihilation of the human race, changes must be made, and the time to make these changes is now. As a race of people, humans are not making the progress they should be; we are just not learning the lessons that have been set for us. The fault lies within our physical body. The brain's thought process is flawed; it is like a computer that is not responding to the commands it is given.

We can change this by altering the way we think. This would correct the problem, but at the moment there just doesn't seem to be the will or the understanding inside us to do this. We are refusing to recognise that there is a problem; we are stuck in a mode that is playing the same thing over and over again and it goes like this:

> *Let's get as much money and as many possessions as we can. Let's keep drinking ourselves silly, it's great. Nobody is going to tell me to stop smoking, even if it is going to kill me. Food is food, isn't it? Anyway, processed food is quick and easy to prepare, and it tastes great. It is also useful to be fat, as it keeps us warm in the winter.*

I could go on. The point here is that, if the human body is faulty and is unable to respond to guidance, it will be disregarded, and it will be a channel that will no longer be available as a method of learning.

Dispensing with money and learning to change our thought processes is the way to go, but are we big enough to accept the challenge? I would say, not at the moment. Few people are listening to the positive information that has been circulating for quite a while now, and very few people are listening to their higher self or the guides who have been assigned to help them. Humans as a race of people are basically drifting around with no purpose at all. While much of the population of the world is linked into the baser aspects of living and there is a need for some people to covet the possessions and indeed the personal information and identity of others, the world will go on much as it has been, slowly sinking into new depths of depravity. Although generally, most people believe that everything is okay and normal, the degeneration of a race of people, which is a slow affair, can proceed almost unnoticed until it reaches a depth that is difficult to recover from.

It doesn't have to be like this. You can start to recognise the oncoming demise by taking the focus away from yourself and beginning to look around you. You will not have to look far to see the degeneracy and the state of moral corruption and discontent that is plaguing our world. Many people just shrug these sightings off as isolated incidents that do not involve them, but isolated incidents have a tendency to increase in number until they become so numerous that they are a common occurrence and regarded as normal. It is these patterns of events that will gradually take us down to an unrecoverable low if we don't do something now.

## Taking action

I will say again: "It doesn't have to be like this." We should be living in paradise now, not in the hell that most of us regard as normal. Everybody has the ability to change his or her life; everybody has the opportunity to live life to the full. All we have to do is agree upon two things: the abolition of money worldwide and the need to change the way we think. We can change the way we think by making some simple lifestyle changes. These have been discussed earlier, but let's go over them again.

## Eating the correct food

Begin by eating good food – that is, food that contains vitamins, minerals, proteins, fatty acids, and other nutrients that our bodies need to stay healthy and the brain needs to function properly. When the brain does not function properly and the mind is plagued by incorrect thoughts, we end up living in the kind of world that we have today. I know that everybody believes they are thinking properly, but take an honest look around you: Is this the world you really want? Is everything that enters your world exactly what you are pleased to see there?

If your mind could have just 30 per cent of focused thoughts – that is, thoughts you actually put there – your world would change dramatically. If everybody had 30 per cent focused thoughts, the whole world would change dramatically. The world that we have here today is a nightmare world; it is time to wake up. It doesn't have to be like this. It is only like this because you have chosen to accept living like this in the world we have today.

## Practicing the correct exercise

In order the stay fit as well as healthy, it is important to exercise daily. Practising the correct exercise is essential. Do not practice extreme forms of exercise; it is better to practice gentle but powerful exercises that do not subject the body to extreme repetitive strain. As mentioned earlier in this book, qigong, t'ai chi, and yoga are gentle but powerful exercises that will keep your body and mind fit. They will help to increase the quantity and flow of chi around the body.

## Breathing correctly

Correct breathing is essential to fuel the body with oxygen and chi, both of these elements are needed by the body – especially the brain – to stay in good working order. Total deprivation of either of these elements will result in death; partial deprivation will affect the workings of the body and the way the brain is able to think.

It is interesting to observe the correlation between how people are thinking now and what is happening in the world today. As mentioned earlier in this book, many if not most people shallow-breathe naturally. This way of breathing partially deprives the body and especially the brain of its required amount of oxygen and chi.

## Relaxing

Being able to relax is also essential. When the body and mind are under stress, learning how to relax will eliminate stress from these areas. Being able to breathe correctly promotes relaxation; when the brain is relaxed, the mind is able to enjoy clear and coherent thoughts. When the mind has clear and coherent thoughts, our world can change from the competitive-thinking world that we are living in now to the creative-thinking world that we should be living in.

## Meditating

Meditation is a useful exercise to practice because it gives the mind focus. A focused mind can maintain concentration levels for long periods of time, making problem-solving and difficult situations that frequently occur much easier to overcome. When you practise meditation, your breathing slows down, allowing your body to relax and thereby eliminating stress. If meditation is practised regularly, the relaxation that you benefit from while meditating will become a part of your life outside of meditation.

When these five "life to the full" components are practised regularly, your body will, over a short period of time, return to balance. When your body becomes balanced, the path that you travel will be less arduous, and this will create the right conditions for your mind to change. This will also change how your mind thinks and what it thinks about. Your life will change in turn from a competitive-thinking life to a creative-thinking life.

When your physical body changes and you begin to settle down into the creative way of living, the choices that you make are influenced by your mind. The mind, when it is fully fuelled, enjoys clarity of thought and a high sustained level of concentration. It will be reluctant to return to the time when it was confused and suffered from poor concentration levels.

The thoughts that are now being produced within the creative mind are of a nature that will keep the body healthy and in good working order. This regime is maintained by the mind guiding the body away from foods that are, in the long term, harmful and addictive, and encouraging healthier options by making them more appealing and in line with the lifestyle you are now living. The body knows what it needs and is drawn to the type of food that brings nutritious, wholesome, and beneficial goodness to itself. When the mind changes in this way, it will influence the body to practice the right type of exercise – the type it needs to stay fit and flexible.

When the mind is in balance with the body once more, the body will no longer be attracted to the wrong foods and will resist becoming undernourished again. Now that your body is fit, healthy, and active, there is no need for it to return to the overweight, sluggish, and unfit body it was before. Did you notice that there was not a drug, an electric wire, or a gun held to the head to accomplish this?

Changing the way we live from a competitive-thinking world to a creative-thinking world can change the future plans for the Earth. Instead of a forced plan of action that is out of our control, we can embrace a controlled plan of action instigated by ourselves for ourselves. We can raise the status of this world to that of a paradise where we would be pleased to come to learn from again and again.

# Chapter 17

# Conclusion

In this concluding chapter, I will give you an idea of how living life to the full could work for you. This is only a guide to show how you might be able to include each element into your life every day to get the best possible benefit. Let us look at how this will work on a day-to-day basis, starting from the beginning of the first day.

**Waking up**

I realise that there are many people reading this book who would like to adopt some, or maybe all, of the elements I've described into their lives but will shudder at the mention of Monday morning. Straight away, you are being confronted by your first hurdle. It is the start of the week and for many people that means going back to work. The dreaded alarm clock has gone off, and it is a struggle to get out of bed.

Okay, so let's stop here. Approaching the day in this way will only cause the Monday morning feeling to stay with you or even escalate throughout the day. Let's start in the same way we mean to go on. It is not necessary to wake up to an alarm clock, even one that plays music or offers an early morning chat program instead of a blaring noise. All of these jangle your nerves as they wrench you from your sleep, and they subconsciously set up the way you are going to feel for the rest of the day. It is easy to change this by learning how to set the alarm clock in your subconscious mind to wake you up naturally and gently.

Here is how it is done:

1. Decide what time you would like to get up in the morning and affirm this time out loud to yourself three times while visualising a picture of this time in your mind. Try not to think of anything else while you are doing this affirmation, as it will draw you away from what you are trying to achieve, and it will not work.

2. When you have finished setting the alarm clock in your head, you must believe completely without any trace of scepticism that what you have just affirmed will definitely work and that whatever time you have set in your mind will without any reservation be the time that you are going wake up in the morning. There must be no doubt at all in your mind that you are going to wake up at the affirmed time, because this is the time you have set for your subconscious mind to wake you up.

3. When you wake up at the time you have stated, you must bring yourself to full consciousness and get up straight away. If you waver in any way and fall back to sleep, there is no snooze button built in. By falling back to sleep, you are sending a negative signal to your subconscious mind that you are not serious about

getting up at the time you have set, so it will no longer wake you up.

4. Repeat the alarm clock affirmation in Step 1 three times a day every day for three days, saying the last affirmation just before you go to bed. Unless you change the time that you want to wake up, you will not have to affirm it any more. It will happen automatically.

Waking up in this way is so much better than with an alarm clock. Your mind is going to be much more alert and your body will feel refreshed after a good night's sleep. When you wake up, express your gratitude for your newfound skill and state that you are really look forward to taking on the day ahead with expectation and enthusiasm. You will feel within you a definite difference when you wake up without having to use a conventional alarm clock.

## Daily routine

Monday through to Sunday, after your morning ablutions but before your breakfast, drink one or two glasses of water. This will start off the day's detoxification process within your body. This is also the right time to do your exercise. To start with, just train for fifteen minutes, practising the correct exercise. You can increase this time when your body feels ready. Your breakfast should be made up of slow-release ingredients that will keep your appetite satisfied until lunchtime. Cornflakes and the like do not fall into this category.

Always leave yourself enough time so that you can arrive at work or an appointment on time without having to rush. While you are at work, although you are in a competitive environment, you must maintain a creative-thinking mind. This will help you to complete all the work you have to do for that day, and you will then be filling the space you occupy. Staying with a creative-thinking mind alleviates any stress and prevents you from competing against your workmates, your boss, or yourself. You will find that your job becomes easier and more enjoyable, and it will leave you open to see any opportunities that may come your way.

Even if you are not working, make sure you fill your day. Do just enough to justify your right to occupy the space you live in. If you are a retired person and do nothing of any consequence, see how quickly somebody else will fill your space. Life lessons are presented to us right up until the time we have to leave this world. Working for financial reward is a human thing, not a universal requirement. Work and lessons come in many guises. Laziness, dropping out, sloth, or intellectual indolence will not give you the right to occupy the space you live in for very long – that is, unless it is a part of your life lesson. Your conscience will let you know if it is or not.

After work, or however you have spent your day, if you were not able to practice meditation in the morning, then early evening before you eat is a good time to get to it. Meditate for just ten minutes per day for a couple of weeks to start off with, and then, when you feel comfortable and are ready to meditate longer, increase this time to fifteen minutes. Continue increasing the length of your meditation until you eventually reach thirty minutes. It is then up to you if you want to increase your meditation time any further. Watching TV is okay for a while each day, but it is best not to make a career of it. There are far more important things to do with your life than watching other people make money by trying to persuade you to spend yours.

Sleep is designed to rejuvenate your body so that it can function properly at the start of a new day. It is important to get enough sleep without having to lie in to catch up on it. Try to make sure you get at least eight hours sleep a night; even though you may feel you can get away with less, you will not be doing yourself any favours because, although your body is able to heal itself twenty-four hours a day, it is especially receptive to healing and repairs when it is resting and at its most relaxed. This happens to most people when they are asleep, so an adequate amount of sleep is important.

Eating is an important part of this schedule. To live your life to the full, eat food that is good for your body. The correct food will fuel every part of your body with the vitamins, minerals, and other essentials it needs to function properly. When your body is fed and watered correctly, you will not feel that you need to eat between meals. Your body knows when it has eaten enough; feed it properly, and it will last you a lifetime without any strain. Eat 80% good healthy food every day. The other 20% leaves you room to indulge in whatever you fancy.

Exercising every day is also essential if you are to live your life to the full. Don't start to practice whatever exercise or sport may be in fashion at the moment, because when it goes out of fashion, you will probably stop doing it. There are many ways to exercise, but the correct exercise is the best. If you have to hang bent over double gasping for breath while trying to slow your heart rate down after you have been exercising, this is probably not the best exercise to be doing. The form of exercise I would recommend for people of any age is either qigong or t'ai chi or both. There are plenty of books and articles about them, or you can find out more online about qigong and t'ai chi and where there are classes you can attend in your area.

Living life to the full is not achieved by attending classes once a week. This form of exercise must to be practised every day to give you the kind of benefit you are expecting to achieve in your life, so take whatever you learn home with you and practice every day. Living life to the full will give you maximum benefit, providing you put into it your maximum effort. By slotting qigong or t'ai chi into your daily schedule, you will quickly obtain these benefits. They can make changes to your life that you would never have dreamed of.

We now come to the two most important items that need to be added to your daily schedule. Without either of these two items, you will not achieve a life that is lived to the full.

## Correct breathing

Breathing correctly is the most important thing that a person can learn to do. I have mentioned this a dozen times or more throughout this book because it is the one thing that will significantly change your life – more than any other element I have mentioned. Breathing in the correct manner can benefit not only the health of your physical body, which is an important priority, but also the functionality of your brain. When working correctly, it is able to retain more information within its memory cells. When the brain receives the correct amount of oxygen it requires, you are then presented with a mind that is in tip top condition and working with crystal clear thinking.

Breathing correctly can also help you to improve and maintain your concentration level for longer periods. When your brain is properly oxygenated and begins to work as it should, it can command the rest of your body to perform tasks more easily, with a reaction time that will be much faster. Breathing correctly all of the time can do all of this for you and a lot more.

## *Total relaxation*

Time to relax is the second most important component of your daily schedule. Relaxation can only be fully achieved when you are able to breathe correctly. I have already expounded on the virtues of total relaxation earlier in this book, but I will mention again that when your body and mind are in a truly relaxed state – not just when you are resting but also when you are active – stress will not be present within your mind or your physical body.

There cannot be two opposing elements occupying the same place at the same time. If you are able to maintain a relaxed disposition throughout the remainder of your life, then the rest of your days will be relatively stress-free. This must surely be a life-changing experience for the better.

## Your head start

How on earth you are going to fit every recommendation from this book into your life? It's easy, because you are doing most of it already.

These are the five main elements that will enable you to live your life to the full when they are practised every day.

1. Breathing
2. Relaxing
3. Eating and drinking

4.  Exercising
5.  Meditating

Let's see how much extra time you're going to need to fit all of these into your day.

### *Breathing*

You already breathe; it is obviously something that everybody must do. It is an essential part of living on this world, so why not breathe correctly? It will not take up any more of your time to do so; in fact, when you breathe correctly, you'll find that it takes little effort compared to shallow breathing. You will also expend less energy by breathing the correct way, so you will be less tired.

When you breathe correctly using the diaphragm muscle, your body and mind begin to relax more easily than they would if you were shallow-breathing; in fact, when you shallow-breathe, you increase the chance of stress in your neck, shoulders, lungs, and head. Not the best way to relax.

### *Relaxing*

You do not need to spend any extra time practising relaxation, as this will come to you naturally when you are breathing correctly. You do not need to sit or lie down specifically to relax, because your body and mind will become naturally relaxed at all times, even when you are moving around. Any stress within you will just melt away. When you are in a state of permanent relaxation, you are able to handle any potentially stressful situations much more easily.

Relaxation changes the way you think. The mind is able to think much more clearly when it is relaxed, and it is able to make a more coherent decision when it is not burdened by the weight of stress. Breathing correctly and being completely relaxed are life-changing elements that are the foundation of living your life to the full. They will not take up any more of your time than they already do.

### Eating and drinking

Our body is the same as any mechanical machine; it needs fuel to animate it. The fact that it is a biomechanical machine makes no difference. We are bioelectrical beings who need to top up with fuel frequently to produce electricity – just like a car or a power station, except that instead of coal or oil, we use food and water. It is logical to assume that to keep our bodies in tip-top condition, we would want to use the best fuel available.

We have only one body, so it makes sense to want to keep it fit, healthy, and looking good. Unfortunately, this does not seem to be the case here in the Western world. In our society, the preferred foods for the majority of people are processed foods because they are cheap to buy, they're quick and easy to cook, and they taste good. Unfortunately, a large proportion of this type of food contains very little fuel for the body.

Everybody must eat and drink, so why not eat and drink the best food and drink you can buy? This is the only body you have, and it has got to last you a lifetime. It takes no longer to eat good-quality food than it does to eat rubbish. In fact, it takes less time, because you won't need to eat it all day long.

## *Exercising*

Exercise is a vital part of living your life to the full, yet the wrong type of exercise can be harmful to the body. It is wise to choose the kind of exercise that is right for your body. When you have chosen what is right for you, do not do it to excess or you might negate any benefits you have gained from doing it. If you do not exercise at the moment, you will have to find the time somewhere in your schedule to fit it in.

## *Meditating*

Meditation is another element of living your life to the full. It is exercise for the mind and gives you the ability to develop focused thought; it will also strengthen and cultivate your ability to achieve deeper relaxation. Such relaxation releases stress from the body and mind, and in so doing gives you the ability to handle with ease any stress that may come along in the future. Meditating can also help you to develop a better understanding of your own spirituality.

As with exercising, if you do not meditate already, it is important to find the time somewhere in your daily schedule.

## Adding it up

Although many elements of living life to the full are described within this book, in this chapter I have revisited only the five most important ones. When these five elements are practised every day, you can easily achieve a life that is lived to the full. Of these five, there are actually only two that you may need to find extra time to practice, because you must already be doing the other three naturally to stay alive. When you add the two remaining elements – exercise and meditation, which when combined will amount to less than an hour of extra practice time to be added to your daily schedule – you will find that this is not a big price to pay for the opportunity of living your life to the full.

## The achievements

I have been writing about how wonderful your life will become when you live it to the full. I shall now tell you exactly what to expect when you really do it.

Your health will start to improve quite quickly when your body begins to detoxify, as you start to drink water every day when you first wake up. Your health will carry on improving as you change your diet to the kind of foods that contain the right nutrition for your body. You will also find that when your body receives the vitamins, minerals, and other essentials it needs, you will not want to eat all day. Your body will be satisfied with just three meals a day, and the way you think about the foods you might want to eat will change.

The fitness of your body is of extreme importance and plays a major part in your life. It determines what kind of life you are able to live. An unfit body that has done little or no exercise could mean that you are only able to live a sedentary lifestyle. If your muscles have become weak through lack of activity, you may also find that you will have to go through a lifetime of ill health because inactivity has weakened your inner foundation and lowered your immune system, keeping you from fighting off disease and illness. Without exercise, your physical body is unlikely to be able to complete all of the lessons that were set out for you in this life, because it is unlikely you will live the full lifespan you were given

When you begin to practice the correct exercise every day, there will be a vast improvement to the fitness of your physical body and, surprisingly, to the function of your brain as well. Your muscles will become stronger, as will your inner foundation. Now that you are active, your immune system can start to rise up and keep illness and disease from striking you down. According to my own experience of daily exercise and living my life to the full, I can truthfully say I am never ill, and my health and fitness have been first-class for many years now.

Exercising every day will make you healthier, happier, fitter, and more flexible. As your mind begins to change what it thinks about, its foremost concern will be for health and fitness. You will not want to stop feeling fit and healthy, so exercising won't become a chore. You will start to look forward to practising every day and even doing more.

Meditation is exercise for the mind. Meditate at least once a day, and after about six months (and this period varies from person to person), your perception of life around you will change. It will change how you see and sense the things that are happening within your life and also outside of your life. You will become aware that you are seeing things from a different perspective. The more you meditate, the greater the understanding of your purpose here on Earth will become. The more you meditate, the more you will want to meditate, and the greater these changes will be.

When you include meditation alongside the other four elements, the achievements you can obtain as you advance towards a life that is lived to the full will be assured. The things that you think about now should in the future change in nature, and the way that your mind now operates could change quite radically also. Your spiritual perception should become much clearer, as will the thoughts within your mind generally. When you begin to meditate more often and for longer periods, relaxation will become your constant companion. Stress will melt away from your life, and your general deportment will be that of a quiet, relaxed person who is respected by others for your wisdom, the manner in which you express yourself, and the inner peace that radiates from you.

It is these ascribed qualities that you will be accredited with when you are living your life to the full. With these achievements, you will be seen as an advancing person. There can be no doubt at all that you are filling the space you occupy, as you must achieve your purpose for coming to this world. For those of you who are not quite there yet, your time will soon come. For those of you who are now ready to move on, I will see you there when you arrive.

# About the Author

In his second book, Raymond G Floodgate shares over forty years of study and practical experience to help and benefit the reader. He is a certificated Reiki master and teacher, a qualified practitioner of energy healing, and an energy healing teacher.

For twelve years, he was a practitioner and instructor of Shotokan karate, but over the last sixteen years he has changed direction from martial activities and treating illness to the prevention of illness. To this end, he has concentrated on the practice and instruction of t'ai chi, qigong, and meditation. He also teaches the art of relaxation and the correct breathing method, and for the past eleven years he has been holding classes, giving talk, and performing demonstrations of the benefit these practices.